THE FLAVORS OF

BON APPÉTIT

2001

THE FLAVORS OF
BON APPÉTIT
2001

from the Editors of Bon Appétit

Condé Nast Books • Clarkson Potter/Publishers

New York

For *Bon Appétit* Magazine

Barbara Fairchild, *Editor-in-Chief*
Laurie Glenn Buckle, *Editor, Bon Appétit Books*
Marcy MacDonald, *Editorial Business Manager*
Carri Marks, *Editorial Production Director*
Sybil Shimazu Neubauer, *Editorial Administrator*
Laura Samuel Meyn, *Assistant Editor*
Marcia Hartmann Lewis, *Editorial Support*
Norman Kolpas, *Text*
H. Abigail Bok, *Copy Editor*
Gaylen Ducker Grody, *Research*
Elizabeth A. Matlin, *Index*

For *Condé Nast* Books

Lisa Faith Phillips, *Vice President and General Manager*
Tom Downing, *Direct Marketing Director*
Deborah Williams, *Associate Operations Director*
Jennifer Zalewski, *Direct Marketing Associate*
Barbara Giordano, *Direct Marketing Assistant*
Eric Levy, *Inventory Assistant*

Design: Ph.D
Production design: Monica Elias

Front Jacket: Orange Cheesecake with Caramel Sauce (page 172)
Facing Page: Top: Cucumber and Avocado Soup (page 31)
           Middle: Cornish Game Hens with Pancetta, Juniper Berries and Beets (page 85)
           Bottom: Lemon-Blueberry Cake with White Chocolate Frosting (page 170)

Published by Clarkson Potter/Publishers, 299 Park Avenue, New York, New York 10171.
Member of the Crown Publishing Group.
Random House, Inc.
New York, Toronto, London, Sydney, Auckland

CLARKSON N. POTTER, POTTER, and colophon are registered trademarks of Random House, Inc.

Printed in the United States of America

Library of Congress Cataloging-in-Publication Data.

The Flavors of Bon Appétit 2001/from the editors of Bon Appétit.
Includes index. 1. Cookery. I. Bon Appétit.
TX714. F59223 2001
641.5—dc21

                           00-065223

ISBN 0-609-60920-3

10 9 8 7 6 5 4 3 2 1

FIRST EDITION

Condé Nast Web Address: http://www.epicurious.com
Condé Nast Books Web Address: http://www.bonappetitbooks.com
Random House Web Address: http://www.randomhouse.com

Contents

Introduction

Every year for eight years now, we at *Bon Appétit* have been devoting the first issue of the year to a fond look back at what has gone on in the food world over the preceding 12 months. Specifically, we zero in on the trends that emerged, highlighting the best of what we saw out there—styles of cooking, types of food, ways of entertaining and such. We follow that issue with a survey, published in March, that summarizes a readers' poll designed to find out, among other things, what you like (and don't like) to eat and how you like to cook and entertain. It's always gratifying when our report on what's new and delicious jibes with what our readers are thinking is new and delicious too.

In this, the eighth volume in The Flavors of Bon Appétit series, the most influential trends of the year and our readers' favorite foods come together to form a very well rounded collection of the kinds of recipes that make for great cooking. Add to that menus that show how easy it is to mix and match the recipes, sidebars that are packed with fascinating information and recipe notes that offer useful tips and advice, and the result is a cookbook for the day and for the decade.

Cherries Simmered in Red Wine
(page 164)

One thing we learned in our most recent survey was just how popular Italian food continued to be with readers. Some 81 percent of respondents listed it as their favorite cuisine to cook at home, while 72 percent declared it their top choice when eating out. This proved especially good news in the face of what was then our upcoming May issue, devoted to the simple, soulful and often surprising cooking of Tuscany. Many of the utterly delicious recipes from that special collector's edition appear here, among them Chicken with Prosciutto and Sage (page 83), Potato-Sausage Tortelli with Ragù (page 118) and Cherries Simmered in Red Wine (page 164).

Chinese food, as might be expected, came in a close second to Italian in popularity. It and other Asian cuisines are generously represented here in recipes ranging from Chinese-Style Steamed Fish (page 91) and Duck Breasts with Orange, Honey and Tea Sauce (page 87) to Spicy Vietnamese Beef and Noodle Soup (page 44) and Ginger Beef Tataki with Lemon-Soy Dipping Sauce (page 48).

Two new ethnic trends (both of which add their own taste of excitement to this volume) punctuated the "best of the year" issue and may, by next year, turn up on the survey as cuisines readers are experimenting with at home. The bold flavors of contem-

Shrimp and Sweet Potato Cakes
with Chipotle Tartar Sauce (page 12)
and Spicy Chayote Slaw (page 138)

porary Latin American cooking, or *nuevo Latino*, are evident in such dishes as Shrimp and Sweet Potato Cakes with Chipotle Tartar Sauce (page 12) and Chicken Marinated in Garlic, Chilies and Citrus Juices (page 74). Hot on that trend's heels is one of the most widely talked-about fusion foods of recent times, the new Indian cooking, represented here in recipes including Curried Scallop and Vegetable Chowder (page 103) and Cinnamon-Clove Ice Cream (page 188).

But despite such globe-trotting tastes, we also know for a fact that our readers still crave all-American standbys (71 percent voted it their favorite cuisine to make at home). To satisfy those homespun cravings, turn to recipes for such satisfying standards as Chicken and

Swiss Chard and Herb Tart
(page 111)

Vegetable Pot Pies with Dilled Biscuit Topping (page 76), Sautéed Shrimp on Parmesan Grits (page 97) and Blueberry Pie with Lattice Crust (page 158).

Hand in hand with that allegiance to our nation's regional foods comes a dedication to outdoor cooking. We know it's a favorite way to entertain, a fact supported by our survey, and just plain obvious when you combine the appeal of eating outside with such great barbecued fare as Chili-rubbed Rib-eye Steaks (page 42), Sweet-and-Smoky Baby Back Ribs with Bourbon Barbecue Sauce (page 66) and Grilled Lobster with Ginger Butter (page 100).

Even as all that grilling indicates a continuing devotion to meat, we're also seeing a rising interest in vegetarian cooking. Whether for reasons of health or of conscience, or simply because more and more people have discovered the pleasures of peak-of-season produce, a good percentage of our readers now say that they are eating meatless entrées on a regular basis. Both part-time and full-time vegetarians will find great satisfaction in the many meat-free main courses that follow, including Swiss Chard and Herb Tart (page 111), Southwestern Tofu Wraps (page 112) and Portobello Burgers with Red Pepper Mayonnaise (page 109).

That last dish suggests yet another trend identified among the top ten: upscale sandwiches. No longer hidden away in lunch bags, sandwiches made with imaginative fillings and artisanal breads now star on menus of top restaurants and bring new inspiration to home cooks. Outstanding examples of this trend include Cal-Asian Seared Tuna Sandwiches (page 90) and Roasted Chicken, Zucchini and Ricotta Sandwiches on Focaccia (page 81).

Roasted Chicken, Zucchini and Ricotta Sandwiches on Focaccia (page 81)

As might be imagined, both our survey results and our report on the trends covered more ground than what has been mentioned here, from the growing popularity of book-club dinner parties to our love of eating hamburgers in the car (75 percent of men and 61 percent of women do it). To give more of our findings their due, we've added a special section at the back of this book that features recipes for our readers' favorite foods. It begins on page 198.

While much of what we learned in our own research and in the survey responses yielded some surprises, it was not at all surprising to discover that desserts are as popular as ever. About four out of every five of our surveyed readers said they eat dessert at least once a week, and almost two-thirds said they actually prepare a dessert once or twice a week. For those who number among that majority, this book offers a wonderfully generous helping of sweet sensations, from Chocolate Crunch Layer Cake with Milk Chocolate Frosting (page 174) and Raspberry-Apricot Shortcakes (page 176) to Coconut Crème Brûlée (page 183) and Hot Lemon Soufflés (page 180).

Desserts, sandwiches, great meatless dishes, barbecue fare, down-home treats, ethnic adventures and Italian dishes you wouldn't expect to find outside Italy—what more could you want in a cookbook? But more there is. . . .

Raspberry-Apricot Shortcakes (page 176)

Wild Mushroom and Leek Galettes
(page 23)

Starters

appetizers

soups

beverages

Shrimp and Sweet Potato Cakes with Chipotle Tartar Sauce

Serve the Spicy Chayote Slaw (page 138) with these shrimp and sweet potato cakes (both pictured at right) to make a complete and delicious first course for a Latin-inspired meal.

LATIN SPICE MIX

- 1/4 cup cumin seeds
- 1 tablespoons whole black peppercorns
- 1 tablespoon coriander seeds
- 2 tablespoons sugar
- 1 1/2 teaspoons sea salt

SHRIMP AND SWEET POTATO CAKES

- 1 pound tan-skinned sweet potatoes
- 4 large garlic cloves, unpeeled
- 4 tablespoons (or more) vegetable oil

- 8 ounces peeled cooked large shrimp, coarsely chopped
- 2/3 cup chopped fresh cilantro
- 2/3 cup panko (Japanese breadcrumbs)*
- 2 tablespoons finely chopped poblano chili**
- 2 tablespoons finely chopped red onion

  All purpose flour

  Chipotle Tartar Sauce (see recipe opposite)

FOR LATIN SPICE MIX: Combine first 3 ingredients in heavy medium skillet. Stir over medium heat until fragrant and toasted. Cool slightly. Finely grind spices in blender. Transfer to small bowl. Mix in sugar and salt.

appetizers

FOR SHRIMP AND SWEET POTATO CAKES: Preheat oven to 350°F. Pierce potatoes all over with fork. Place on baking sheet. Toss garlic with 1 tablespoon oil in small bowl. Enclose garlic in foil; place on baking sheet with potatoes. Bake until potatoes and garlic are tender, about 30 minutes for garlic and 1 hour 15 minutes for potatoes. Cool garlic and potatoes slightly. Remove peel from garlic. Remove skins from potatoes. Mash potatoes and garlic in bowl until smooth.

Add next 5 ingredients and 1½ teaspoons Latin spice mix (reserve remaining spice mix for use in Spicy Chayote Slaw, page 138, or for another use) to mashed potato mixture. Stir to blend well. Season with salt. Form mixture into six 3-inch-diameter patties.

Preheat oven to 375°F. Lightly coat cakes in flour. Heat remaining 3 tablespoons oil in heavy large skillet over medium-high heat. Cook cakes in batches until brown, adding more oil if necessary, about 2 minutes per side. Place on baking sheet. Bake until heated through, 5 minutes.

Place 1 cake on each plate. Spoon sauce atop cakes and serve.

Panko, Japanese breadcrumbs, are available in Asian markets and in the Asian foods section of some supermarkets.
**A fresh green chili, often called a pasilla, available at Latin American markets and also at some supermarkets nationwide.*

6 SERVINGS

Chipotle Tartar Sauce

- 1 cup mayonnaise
- 2 tablespoons drained capers, chopped
- 2 tablespoons chopped cornichons, gherkins or dill pickles
- 1½ tablespoons fresh lime juice
- 1 tablespoon minced canned chipotle chilies*

Mix all ingredients in medium bowl to blend. Season to taste with salt.

Chipotle chilies canned in a spicy tomato sauce, sometimes called adobo, are available at Latin American markets, specialty foods stores and some supermarkets nationwide.

MAKES 1¼ CUPS

Shopping for
Nuevo Latino Flavors

Nuevo Latino cuisine is one of the biggest trends to hit the restaurant scene in years. A vibrant mixing and matching of ingredients and dishes, it incorporates influences from Cuba and Mexico to Central and South America. The result is food with a bold combination of flavors.

As awareness of the cuisine grows, the products that make it special are beginning to be sold in supermarkets. Keep your eyes open for the following nuevo Latino standbys.

- Chayote: Resembling a pear, this fruit has a cucumber-like taste and texture; it's also known as vegetable pear, mirliton or christophine.
- *Chipotle* Chilies: The dried, smoked form of jalapeño chilies, these are often sold canned in a spicy tomato sauce, which is sometimes called *adobo*.
- Coconut Milk: This flavorful milky liquid is produced by grating coconut meat, combining it with water and straining it. It's sold in cans; don't confuse it with canned sweetened cream of coconut.
- Jalapeño Chilies: These green or ripened red fresh chilies are two to three inches long, with thick, moderately hot flesh.
- Poblano Chilies: Fresh dark-green tapered chilies, often called *pasillas*, that are four to five inches long and medium to hot in flavor.

Vegetable Tart with Basil

This savory tart makes a great starter for an Italian-style meal—or serve it as a meatless entrée with a salad and bread for a light lunch. If you're short on time, substitute a purchased, refrigerated pie crust for the homemade one here.

CRUST

1³/₄ cups all purpose flour
¹/₂ teaspoon salt
¹/₂ cup (1 stick) chilled unsalted butter, cut into ¹/₂-inch cubes
4 tablespoons (about) ice water

FILLING

2 tablespoons (¹/₄ stick) butter
2 tablespoons olive oil
3 cups coarsely chopped mixed red, yellow and green bell peppers
1 cup ¹/₂-inch pieces eggplant
1 cup ¹/₂-inch pieces carrots
1 cup ¹/₂-inch pieces onion
2 tablespoons tomato paste
¹/₃ cup chopped fresh basil

FOR CRUST: Mix flour and salt in processor. Add butter; cut in using on/off turns until coarse meal forms. Gradually blend in enough ice water by table-spoonfuls to form moist clumps. Gather dough into ball; flatten into disk. Wrap in plastic and refrigerate 1 hour. *(Can be prepared 2 days ahead. Keep refrigerated. Soften slightly before rolling out.)*

Preheat oven to 375°F. Roll out dough on lightly floured surface to 13-inch round. Transfer to 9-inch-diameter tart pan with removable bottom. Trim overhang to ³/₄ inch. Fold overhang in, forming double-thick sides. Pierce crust all over with fork. Freeze 15 minutes. Bake until golden brown, about 35 minutes. Cool on rack. Maintain oven temperature.

FOR FILLING: Melt butter with oil in large skillet over medium-high heat. Add vegetables, cover and cook 5 minutes, stirring occasionally. Uncover; sauté until almost tender, about 5 minutes. Add tomato paste and basil; sauté 5 minutes. Season to taste with salt and pepper.

Spoon filling into crust. Bake until heated through, about 5 minutes. Cut tart into wedges and serve warm.

8 SERVINGS

Watermelon-Honeydew Kebabs with Lime-Poppy Seed Dressing

3 tablespoons fresh lime juice

3 tablespoons sugar

$1^1/_2$ teaspoons poppy seeds

$^1/_4$ teaspoon salt

$^1/_2$ cup vegetable oil

2 3-pound honeydew melons, halved, seeded

1 small seedless watermelon, cut into $^3/_4$-inch-thick slices

24 6-inch bamboo skewers

Pretty and refreshing, this starter requires no cooking. The poppy seed dressing can be drizzled over the kebabs or served on the side for finicky eaters (like kids).

Whisk first 4 ingredients in medium bowl. Gradually whisk in oil.

Using large melon baller, scoop out 72 balls of honeydew melon. Using $1^1/_4$-inch round fluted cookie cutter, cut out 48 rounds from watermelon slices. Alternate 3 honeydew balls and 2 watermelon rounds on each skewer. *(Can be prepared 4 hours ahead. Cover dressing and kebabs separately and refrigerate.)* Serve kebabs with dressing.

MAKES 24

If you don't want to fire up the grill, make the chips by cutting each pita into six wedges and baking them at 350°F until lightly toasted, about ten minutes. Substitute purchased hummus or pesto for one of the recipes here if you're short on time.

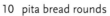

10 pita bread rounds
    Creole-Style Hummus (see recipe opposite)
    Tomatillo, Corn and Olive Salsa (see recipe opposite)
    Lemon Pesto (see recipe opposite)

Prepare barbecue (medium-high heat). Grill pita bread until lightly toasted, turning occasionally, about 4 minutes. Cut each pita into 6 wedges. Place dips on platter. Serve with pita chips.

12 SERVINGS

Creole-Style Hummus

2   15¹/₂-ounce cans garbanzo beans (chickpeas), drained
¹/₂ cup olive oil
¹/₂ cup tahini (sesame seed paste)*
¹/₂ cup water
¹/₄ cup fresh lemon juice
3   garlic cloves
1   teaspoon Creole seasoning blend
1   teaspoon ground cumin

Puree all ingredients in processor until smooth. Transfer to serving bowl. *(Can be made 2 days ahead. Cover and refrigerate.)*

Tahini is available at Middle Eastern markets, natural foods stores and some supermarkets nationwide.

MAKES ABOUT 3³/₄ CUPS

Tomatillo, Corn and Olive Salsa

2   cups frozen corn kernels, thawed
1¹/₂ cups purchased salsa verde
³/₄ cup chopped onion
¹/₂ cup chopped drained jalapeño-stuffed olives
¹/₄ cup chopped fresh parsley

Mix all ingredients in large bowl. Season to taste with salt and pepper. *(Can be made 1 day ahead. Cover and refrigerate.)*

MAKES ABOUT 3 CUPS

Lemon Pesto

3   cups (packed) fresh basil leaves
³/₄ cup freshly grated Parmesan cheese (about 2¹/₂ ounces)
¹/₂ cup olive oil
¹/₂ cup pine nuts
3   tablespoons fresh lemon juice
2   large garlic cloves
1   teaspoon grated lemon peel

Puree all ingredients in processor. Season to taste with salt and pepper. *(Can be made 2 days ahead. Transfer pesto to bowl. Press plastic wrap onto surface of pesto. Cover and refrigerate.)*

MAKES ABOUT 1¹/₂ CUPS

Lunch in the Back Yard for Twelve

Grilled Pita Chips with Three Dips
(opposite; pictured opposite)

Shrimp Remoulade with Avocado and Hearts of Palm
(page 102)

Grilled Lamb Kebabs with Cumin and Cinnamon
(page 57; double recipe)

Iced Tea with Mint, Lemon and Orange

Pound Cake with Fresh Fruit and Bourbon Whipped Cream
(page 173)

Comparing Olive Oils

The International Olive Oil Council in Madrid sets the standards for olive oils, which are rated based on their acidity, taste, aroma and color. Virgin olive oils are from the first press of olives. Extra-virgin olive oil is the best, containing less than 1 percent acidity and a superior taste and aroma, in colors ranging from gold to dark green; a deeper color indicates a more intense olive flavor. They run the gamut from supermarket varieties to specialty oils produced in small batches from hand-picked, organic olives—and the prices range accordingly. Extra-virgin olive oils are best used uncooked, such as in salads, drizzled over pasta or swirled into soup.

One step below is virgin olive oil, which contains less than 3.3 percent acidity. Virgin oils are lighter in color and flavor, and are fine for many uses, including sautéing. If an olive oil has any defects that keep it from qualifying as extra-virgin or virgin, it can be rendered neutral and sold under the name light olive oil—light in taste, not in calories or fat. This version is good for deep-frying. Neutralized oil may also be mixed with up to 25 percent extra-virgin olive oil and sold simply as olive oil.

Fresh Vegetable Platter with Olive Oil Dip

Assorted cut-up vegetables (such as carrots, cucumbers, red bell peppers, yellow bell peppers, cherry tomatoes, fennel bulbs, green onions and radishes)
Extra-virgin olive oil
Sea salt
Crusty Italian bread
Paper-thin prosciutto slices

Arrange vegetables on platter. Allow guests to drizzle oil onto their plates and season oil to taste with salt. Serve with vegetables, bread and prosciutto.

Crab Cakes with Creamy Caper Sauce

CAPER SAUCE

   1 cup mayonnaise

$^1/_2$ cup drained capers, chopped

$^1/_2$ cup chopped fresh parsley

$^1/_2$ cup chopped fresh chives

   2 tablespoons extra-virgin olive oil

   1 tablespoon fresh lemon juice

CRAB CAKES

$1^1/_2$ pounds crabmeat

$3^1/_2$ cups fresh breadcrumbs made from crustless French bread

$^1/_4$ cup chopped fresh parsley

$^1/_4$ cup spicy brown mustard

$^1/_4$ cup mayonnaise

   1 large egg, beaten to blend

   2 teaspoons Old Bay seasoning

$^1/_2$ cup (or more) vegetable oil

Lots of fresh crabmeat and a tangy homemade sauce make these crab cakes delicious and different. Note that the caper sauce can be made ahead, and the crab cakes can be formed ahead, leaving only the frying to do at the last minute.

FOR CAPER SAUCE: Whisk all ingredients in medium bowl to blend. *(Can be made 2 days ahead. Cover and refrigerate.)*

FOR CRAB CAKES: Combine crabmeat, 1 cup breadcrumbs and next 5 ingredients in bowl. Spread remaining $2^1/_2$ cups breadcrumbs on baking sheet. Form crab mixture by $^1/_4$ cupfuls into 24 small balls. Flatten slightly; coat with breadcrumbs. Transfer to another baking sheet. Cover; chill at least 2 hours and up to 1 day.

Heat $^1/_2$ cup vegetable oil in heavy large skillet over medium-high heat. Working in batches, fry crab cakes until brown, adding more oil to skillet as needed, about 4 minutes per side. Transfer 2 crab cakes to each of 12 plates. Serve, passing caper sauce alongside.

12 SERVINGS

Crispy Bruschetta with Goat Cheese, Tomatoes and Mint

Mint is a refreshing change from the usual basil in this *bruschetta* recipe, which makes a great beginning to any Italian-themed meal. Cut down on last-minute preparation by toasting the bread slices and making the tomato mixture ahead of time.

12 $1/2$-inch-thick slices Italian or French bread (from about 3-inch-diameter loaf)
3 tablespoons olive oil
1 large garlic clove, halved

6 plum tomatoes, seeded, chopped
1 teaspoon fresh lemon juice

4 ounces soft fresh goat cheese (such as Montrachet)
3 tablespoons chopped fresh mint

Preheat oven to 325°F. Arrange bread slices on baking sheet. Brush olive oil over both sides of bread. Bake bread until golden, about 6 minutes per side. Remove toasts from oven. Rub cut sides of garlic over toasts.

Combine tomatoes and lemon juice in medium bowl. Season with generous amount of salt and pepper. Toss to combine. *(Can be prepared 1 hour ahead. Cover separately and keep at room temperature.)*

Preheat oven to 350°F. Spread cheese over toasts; arrange on baking sheet. Mound tomatoes on toasts. Bake until heated through, about 8 minutes. Transfer to platter. Sprinkle with mint and serve.

6 SERVINGS

Asparagus, Parmesan and Prosciutto Bundles

18 thin asparagus spears, each trimmed to 7 inches

18 very thin prosciutto slices
18 $2^3/_4$x$^1/_3$x$^1/_3$-inch sticks of Parmesan cheese (about 5 ounces total)

Cut each asparagus spear in half. Cook asparagus pieces in boiling salted water until crisp-tender, about 3 minutes. Drain. Transfer to bowl of ice water. Drain again. Pat asparagus dry.

Lay prosciutto on work surface. Place 1 asparagus piece with tip, 1 asparagus piece without tip and 1 cheese stick crosswise atop 1 short end of each prosciutto slice. Roll up prosciutto to enclose asparagus and cheese. *(Can be made 1 day ahead. Store airtight in refrigerator.)*

6 SERVINGS

Citrus-marinated Olives

1¹/₂ cups Kalamata olives or other brine-cured black olives
1¹/₂ cups cracked brine-cured green olives
1 cup olive oil
¹/₄ cup chopped fresh cilantro
¹/₄ cup fresh lemon juice
¹/₄ cup orange juice
6 large garlic cloves, thinly sliced
3 tablespoons chopped fresh parsley
1 tablespoon grated lemon peel
1 tablespoon grated orange peel
¹/₂ teaspoon dried crushed red pepper

These easy-to-make marinated olives are great to take along on a picnic. They would also be good as an appetizer with cocktails at home.

Combine all ingredients in large heavy-duty resealable plastic bag. Shake bag to blend ingredients. Refrigerate at least 1 day and up to 3 days, turning bag occasionally. Transfer olives and some marinade to bowl. Let stand 1 hour at room temperature before serving.

MAKES ABOUT 3 CUPS

Giving Peppercorns the Grind

When it comes to pepper, nothing beats the flavor of freshly ground peppercorns. Choose a mill that grinds easily, fills without too much fuss, and adjusts to produce everything from powdery pepper to coarse, almost cracked pepper. This range means that one good mill can subtly season egg dishes—or add a distinctive bite to Artichokes with Romano, Cracked Pepper and Olive Oil (at right) and other dishes.

A well-stocked supermarket spice shelf will present a range of choices in whole peppercorns ready for the grinder. Black peppercorns are the most common, picked slightly underripe and sun-dried until the hulls shrivel and oxidize to a black color. White peppercorns, from the same plant, are picked when fully ripe and hulled before drying; they have a subtler, less sharp taste. (Green peppercorns are the same berries picked before they ripen, and are usually preserved without being dried; they should not go into the pepper mill.) Dried pink peppercorns are actually berries that come from an unrelated plant; they add a distinctively sharp, pungent flavor all their own.

Artichokes with Romano, Cracked Pepper and Olive Oil

    2   lemons, halved
    4   artichokes (about 10 ounces each)
  3/4   cup extra-virgin olive oil
  3/4   cup grated pecorino Romano cheese
 1 1/2 teaspoons cracked black pepper
  3/4   teaspoon salt

Squeeze juice from lemon halves into large bowl of cold water; add squeezed lemons. Cut off stem and top 3/4 inch of 1 artichoke and discard. Using scissors, trim sharp tips from leaves. Place artichoke in lemon water until ready to cook. Repeat with remaining artichokes.

Drain artichokes and cook in large pot of boiling salted water until base of each is tender when pierced with knife and leaves pull away easily, about 25 minutes. Drain well. *(Can be made 8 hours ahead. Cover and refrigerate. Steam artichokes 10 minutes to rewarm before continuing.)*

Mix olive oil, pecorino Romano cheese, 1 1/2 teaspoons pepper and 3/4 teaspoon salt in small bowl to blend. Gently press artichoke leaves outward from center to open artichokes slightly. Pull out small purple-tipped leaves, then scoop out fibrous choke. Place 1 artichoke on each of 4 plates. Sprinkle artichoke cavities with salt and pepper. Drizzle 1 tablespoon cheese dressing over each artichoke. Divide remaining cheese dressing equally among 4 small ramekins; serve cheese dressing with artichokes.

4 SERVINGS

Wild Mushroom and Leek Galettes

1   $^3/_4$-ounce package dried chanterelle mushrooms

4   tablespoons ($^1/_2$ stick) butter
$^1/_2$ cup minced leek (white and pale green parts only)
1   large shallot, chopped
6   ounces portobello mushrooms, stems and gills removed, caps finely chopped
$^1/_2$ cup dry white wine
6   tablespoons soft fresh goat cheese (such as Montrachet)
3   tablespoons minced fresh parsley

1   sheet frozen puff pastry (half of 17.3-ounce package), thawed

Dried chanterelle mushrooms and fresh portobello mushrooms combine in the filling for these elegant first-course tarts.

Place dried chanterelles in small bowl. Pour enough hot water over to cover chanterelles; let stand until softened, about 30 minutes. Drain. Finely chop.

Melt 2 tablespoons butter in large nonstick skillet over medium-high heat. Add leek and shallot; sauté 2 minutes. Add 2 tablespoons butter, then portobellos and chanterelles; sauté until tender, about 5 minutes. Add wine; simmer until liquid is reduced by half, about 2 minutes. Add 2 tablespoons goat cheese; stir until slightly thickened, about 1 minute. Season with salt and pepper. Stir in 2 tablespoons parsley. Remove from heat.

Position rack in center of oven; preheat to 375°F. Line baking sheet with parchment paper. Roll out puff pastry sheet on floured surface to 12x12-inch square. Using 4-inch-diameter biscuit cutter or bowl as guide, cut out 4 pastry rounds. Using small cookie cutters, such as those with leaf shape, cut out decorative designs from remaining pastry, if desired. Place rounds on baking sheet, spacing apart. Spread 1 tablespoon goat cheese atop each. Spread mushroom mixture evenly atop each to within $^1/_2$ inch of edge, dividing equally. Turn pastry edges upward slightly to hold topping in place. Place pastry cutouts on baking sheet around galettes.

Bake until pastry is puffed and golden, about 15 minutes for decorative cutouts and 30 minutes for galettes.

Sprinkle galettes with remaining 1 tablespoon minced parsley. Top with pastry cutouts, if desired. Serve immediately.

4 SERVINGS

Deviled Eggs with Tarragon and Capers

For a special touch, spoon the mashed egg yolk mixture into a pastry bag and pipe it into the hard-boiled egg whites. The light versions of mayonnaise and sour cream would also work in this recipe.

6   hard-boiled eggs, peeled, halved lengthwise
3   tablespoons sour cream
2   tablespoons mayonnaise
2   teaspoons fresh lemon juice
$^1/_4$ teaspoon dry mustard
2   tablespoons minced green onion
4   teaspoons drained capers
1   teaspoon minced fresh tarragon

Spoon yolks from egg halves into small bowl; mash yolks to smooth paste. Add sour cream, mayonnaise, lemon juice and mustard; blend well. Mix in green onion, capers and tarragon. Season to taste with salt and pepper. Spoon yolk mixture back into whites, mounding in center. *(Can be made 8 hours ahead. Cover; refrigerate.)*

6 SERVINGS

Guacamole with Tomatoes, Cilantro and Jalapeños

4   large ripe avocados, peeled, pitted
$^1/_2$ cup finely chopped onion
$^1/_2$ cup chopped seeded plum tomatoes
$^1/_2$ cup chopped fresh cilantro
1   4-ounce can diced mild green chilies, drained
1   to 2 teaspoons finely chopped seeded jalapeño chilies

Coarsely mash avocados in large bowl. Mix in onion, tomatoes, cilantro and canned chilies. Mix in jalapeños to taste. Season with salt and pepper. Transfer to serving bowl. *(Can be prepared 4 hours ahead. Place plastic wrap directly onto surface of guacamole. Refrigerate.)*

8 SERVINGS

Shrimp Tempura with Lemon and Olive Mayonnaise

Corn oil (for deep-frying)
$^3/_4$ cup (or more) ice water
1 large egg
Pinch of salt
$^3/_4$ cup unbleached all purpose flour
24 uncooked large shrimp (about 1 pound), peeled, deveined, butterflied

Lemon and Olive Mayonnaise (see recipe below)

Pour enough oil into heavy large pot to reach depth of 3 inches. Heat oil over medium-high heat to 380°F. Whisk $^3/_4$ cup ice water, egg and pinch of salt in medium bowl until frothy. Add flour and stir with whisk just until blended and small lumps remain.

Working in batches, immediately dip shrimp into tempura batter to coat; shake excess batter back into bowl. Add shrimp to hot oil and fry until shrimp curl and coating is crisp, about 3 minutes. Using tongs, transfer shrimp to paper towels; drain. Sprinkle with salt.

Transfer shrimp tempura to platter; serve shrimp immediately with Lemon and Olive Mayonnaise.

6 SERVINGS

Lemon and Olive Mayonnaise

$^3/_4$ cup mayonnaise
2 tablespoons chopped pimiento-stuffed green olives
2 tablespoons minced preserved lemon (peel only)* or
    $1^1/_2$ teaspoons grated lemon peel
$^1/_2$ teaspoon hot pepper sauce

Stir all ingredients in small bowl to blend. Season with black pepper. *(Can be made 1 day ahead. Cover and refrigerate.)*

Lemon preserved in a lemon juice and salt brine is used most often in Moroccan cuisine. Available at some specialty foods stores.

MAKES ABOUT 1 CUP

Fearless Frying

You don't need an industrial-style deep-fryer to fry like a chef. Follow these tips for professional results.

- Cookware: Use a pot or deep-fryer that transfers and retains heat well; it should be deep enough to hold several inches of oil and wide enough to hold food without overcrowding.

- Utensils: A long-handled wire skimmer or slotted metal spoon is perfect for turning and lifting out fried food. Use long metal tongs with insulated handles for unwieldy items. A deep-frying thermometer helps you regulate the temperature.

- Oil or Fat: Canola and other relatively flavorless vegetable oils are good choices for frying. Rendered lard or beef suet contributes richness to some foods. Do not reuse oil or fat; repeated heatings cause it to break down, reducing the temperature to which it can be heated.

- Temperature: Most recipes call for deep-frying temperatures from 350° to 375°F. Thin foods like french fries are fried at a higher temperature because the inside cooks through quickly. Thicker foods, such as chicken wings, are fried at a lower temperature to keep the outside from burning before the inside cooks. Clip a deep-frying thermometer inside the pot; immerse the bulb in the oil without letting it touch the bottom of the pot.

Lentil Soup with Mustard Oil and Tomato-Chive Topping

Pungent Indian spices, along with celery, onion, carrot, tomatoes and broth, transform plain lentils into a delicious and flavorful soup. It keeps for two days in the refrigerator.

3	tablespoons vegetable oil
2	large celery stalks, chopped
1	cup chopped onion
1	small carrot, chopped
2	garlic cloves, chopped
1	tablespoon chopped peeled fresh ginger
4	whole cloves
1^1/$_2$	teaspoons cumin seeds
1^1/$_2$	teaspoons whole coriander seeds
1	small dried chili (such as chili de árbol*), broken in half
7	large plum tomatoes, 4 coarsely chopped, 3 finely chopped
^{1}/$_4$	teaspoon ground turmeric
5	cups canned vegetable broth
1^1/$_2$	cups red lentils**
^{1}/$_3$	cup chopped chives
2	tablespoons mustard seeds

Heat 1 tablespoon oil in heavy large pot over medium heat. Add next 9 ingredients; sauté until vegetables begin to brown, about 12 minutes. Add 4 coarsely chopped tomatoes and turmeric; stir 2 minutes. Add broth and lentils; bring to boil. Reduce heat to medium-low; cover and simmer until lentils are very tender, about 45 minutes. Season to taste with salt and pepper. Puree soup in batches in blender. Return to pot. *(Can be made 2 days ahead. Chill until cold, then cover and keep chilled. Rewarm soup before continuing.)*

Mix 3 finely chopped tomatoes and chives in bowl. Heat 2 tablespoons oil in heavy medium saucepan over medium-high heat. Add mustard seeds; cook until seeds darken and begin to pop, about 2 minutes. Pour into bowl.

Ladle soup into bowls. Top with mustard oil and tomato-chive mixture.

*Available at Latin American markets and some specialty foods stores.
**Available at Indian markets and some supermarkets. If unavailable, use green lentils and simmer about 30 minutes.

6 SERVINGS

Fava Bean and Spring Vegetable Soup

  1   tablespoon olive oil
  2   large leeks (white and pale green parts only), thinly sliced (about 3 cups)
$^1/_2$ cup chopped peeled carrot
$4^1/_2$ cups canned low-salt chicken broth or vegetable broth
  2   cups shelled fresh fava beans (from about 2 pounds unshelled) or one
        10-ounce package frozen baby lima beans, thawed
  5   ounces green beans, trimmed, cut into 1-inch pieces
  8   ounces asparagus, tough ends trimmed, spears cut diagonally
        into 1-inch pieces
$^2/_3$ cup thinly sliced fresh basil
      Freshly grated Parmesan cheese (optional)

Note that you can use frozen baby lima beans (with the same great result) instead of the fresh favas, which can be hard to find if they're out of season. (Favas are available in the spring and early summer.)

Heat oil in heavy large saucepan over medium heat. Add leeks and carrot; sauté until vegetables are tender but not brown, about 8 minutes. Add broth and bring to boil. Add favas and green beans and simmer until almost tender, about 8 minutes. Add asparagus and $^1/_3$ cup basil and simmer until all vegetables are very tender, about 7 minutes longer. Season soup with salt and pepper. Stir in $^1/_3$ cup basil. Ladle soup into bowls. Serve, passing Parmesan separately, if desired.

6 SERVINGS

Black Bean Soup with Cumin and Cilantro

The seeds and ribs are the hottest part of jalapeños and other chilies; including them in this soup gives it an extra kick. Garnish each serving with a cooling dollop of sour cream, if you like.

2 tablespoons olive oil
1¹/₂ cups chopped onions
8 garlic cloves, chopped
¹/₄ cup chopped jalapeños with seeds
2 cups dried black beans (about 13 ounces)
1 tablespoon ground cumin
2 teaspoons ground coriander
8 cups (or more) vegetable stock or canned vegetable broth
1 cup coarsely chopped fresh cilantro

Lime wedges

Heat oil in heavy large pot over medium-high heat. Add onions, garlic and jalapeños; sauté 5 minutes. Mix in beans and spices. Add 8 cups stock and bring to boil. Reduce heat, cover and simmer until beans are tender, stirring occasionally, about 2 hours 15 minutes. Working in batches, puree soup with cilantro in blender. Return soup to pot. Season to taste with salt and pepper. *(Can be prepared 1 day ahead. Cool slightly. Refrigerate uncovered until cold, then cover and keep chilled.)*

Bring soup to simmer, thinning with more stock if necessary. Ladle into bowls. Serve, passing lime wedges separately.

8 SERVINGS

Curried Spinach Soup with Yogurt and Cilantro

Not only is this soup flavorful and appealing—it's good for you, too. It has just 186 calories, 5 grams of fat (only 1 gram is saturated fat) and 5 milligrams of cholesterol per serving.

1 tablespoon olive oil
2 large leeks (white and pale green parts only), chopped
1 tablespoon plus 2¹/₂ cups water
2 teaspoons curry powder
2 small white potatoes, peeled, cut into ¹/₂-inch pieces (about 10 ounces)
1 teaspoon salt
4 cups (packed) fresh baby spinach leaves (about 4 ounces)

2 cups low-fat (1%) milk

¹/₂ cup plain nonfat yogurt
¹/₄ cup chopped fresh cilantro

Heat oil in heavy large saucepan over medium heat. Add leeks and 1 tablespoon water; sauté until leeks are tender, about 5 minutes. Add curry powder and stir 30 seconds. Add remaining 2½ cups water, potatoes and salt and bring to boil. Reduce heat, cover and simmer until potatoes are tender, about 10 minutes. Stir in spinach; simmer until just wilted, about 1 minute. Cool slightly.

Working in batches, puree soup in blender until almost smooth. Return soup to same saucepan. Add milk and bring to simmer. Season soup to taste with salt and pepper.

Ladle soup into 4 bowls. Whisk yogurt until smooth. Swirl 2 tablespoons yogurt into each bowl. Sprinkle with cilantro and serve.

4 SERVINGS

Tomato Soup with Lemon-Rosemary Cream

¼	cup (½ stick) butter
1	onion, finely chopped
2	carrots, peeled, finely chopped
3	garlic cloves, minced
½	teaspoon dried thyme
½	teaspoon dried crushed red pepper
1	bay leaf
2	28-ounce cans crushed tomatoes with added puree
6	cups canned low-salt chicken broth
½	cup whipping cream
¾	teaspoon minced fresh rosemary
2	teaspoons finely grated lemon peel

Minced fresh rosemary and grated lemon peel are whisked with whipping cream until slightly thickened for the attractive garnish.

Melt butter in heavy large saucepan over medium heat. Add onion and next 5 ingredients. Cover; cook until onion is tender, stirring occasionally, about 5 minutes. Add tomatoes and broth. Cover and simmer vegetables 40 minutes. Discard bay leaf. Season to taste with salt and pepper. *(Can be made 2 days ahead. Cool slightly. Cover; chill. Rewarm before continuing.)*

Whisk cream, rosemary and ½ teaspoon lemon peel in bowl until slightly thickened. Season to taste with salt and pepper.

Stir remaining 1½ teaspoons lemon peel into soup. Ladle soup into bowls. Drizzle cream mixture over and serve immediately.

8 SERVINGS

Cucumber and Avocado Soup

    1 large English hothouse cucumber, peeled, diced (about 2$\frac{1}{2}$ cups)
2$\frac{1}{2}$ cups low-fat (1%) buttermilk
    1 avocado, quartered, pitted, peeled
    4 tablespoons chopped red onion
    2 tablespoons chopped fresh basil
  $\frac{1}{2}$ cup seeded chopped tomato
    2 teaspoons fresh lime juice
    4 tablespoons plain nonfat yogurt

Combine cucumber and buttermilk in blender. Chop $\frac{1}{4}$ of avocado; set aside for salad. Add remaining avocado to blender; then add 2 tablespoons red onion and 1 tablespoon basil. Blend until very smooth. Season with salt and pepper. Cover; chill until cold, about 1 hour.

Mix reserved avocado, 2 tablespoons onion, 1 tablespoon basil, tomato and lime juice in bowl. *(Can be made 1 day ahead. Cover separately; chill.)* Ladle soup into 4 bowls. Top with yogurt and tomato salad.

4 SERVINGS

Butternut Squash Soup with Pancetta and Tomatoes

    5 ounces pancetta, coarsely chopped
    2 medium onions, coarsely chopped
  $\frac{1}{4}$ teaspoon dried crushed red pepper
    1 2-pound butternut squash, peeled, seeded, cut into $\frac{1}{2}$-inch dice (about 4 cups)
    2 tablespoons chopped fresh oregano
7$\frac{1}{2}$ cups canned low-salt chicken broth
    2 cups canned diced Italian-style tomatoes with juices
  $\frac{3}{4}$ cup yellow cornmeal

Cook first 3 ingredients in heavy large saucepan over medium-low heat until onions are very soft, stirring occasionally, 10 minutes. Add squash and oregano; cook until squash is crisp-tender, stirring occasionally, 8 minutes. Add broth and tomatoes with juices; bring to boil. Gradually whisk in cornmeal. Reduce heat to medium and simmer until squash is tender, stirring occasionally, about 35 minutes. Season with salt and pepper and serve.

8 TO 10 SERVINGS

Meatless Lunch for Four

Cucumber and Avocado Soup
(at left; pictured opposite)

Southwestern Tofu Wraps
(page 112)

Lemonade

Ginger Spice Cookies
(page 196)

Coffee or Black Tea

Crispy baked strips of tortilla, along with avocado and cilantro, top bowls of this spicy and delicious soup.

6 6-inch-diameter corn tortillas
  Nonstick vegetable oil spray
1 teaspoon chili powder

1 poblano chili*

1 teaspoon cumin seeds

2 tablespoons vegetable oil
$^1/_2$ cup finely chopped onion
2 garlic cloves, minced
3 14$^1/_2$-ounce cans vegetable broth
1 14$^1/_2$-ounce can diced tomatoes in juice
1 tablespoon fresh lime juice

1 ripe avocado, pitted, peeled, cubed
$^1/_4$ cup chopped fresh cilantro

Preheat oven to 350°F. Cut 2 tortillas into matchstick-size strips. Arrange strips on baking sheet; spray with nonstick spray. Sprinkle with chili powder; toss. Bake until crisp, about 15 minutes. Set aside.

Char poblano chili over gas flame or in broiler until blackened on all sides. Enclose in plastic bag 10 minutes. Peel, seed and finely chop chili.

Stir cumin seeds in heavy small skillet over medium-low heat until fragrant, about 4 minutes. Transfer to spice grinder; process until finely ground.

Cut 4 tortillas into 1-inch pieces. Heat oil in large saucepan over medium heat. Add tortilla pieces; cook until crisp and golden, stirring occasionally, about 15 minutes. Add poblano chili, onion and garlic; sauté 2 minutes. Add broth, tomatoes with juices and cumin. Simmer gently over medium-low heat 20 minutes. Stir in lime juice. Season with salt and pepper. *(Can be made 8 hours ahead. Cover; chill. Rewarm before serving.)*

Ladle soup into bowls. Garnish with avocado, cilantro and tortilla strips.

*A fresh green chili, often called a pasilla, available at Latin American markets and also some supermarkets nationwide.

6 SERVINGS

Fresh Asparagus Soup

$^1/_2$ cup (1 stick) butter

4 medium onions, chopped

$6^1/_2$ cups (about) canned low-salt chicken broth

3 pounds fresh asparagus, trimmed, tips reserved, stalks coarsely chopped, or three 10-ounce packages frozen asparagus spears, unthawed

Sour cream

Melt butter in heavy large pot over medium-high heat. Add onions; sauté until tender, about 10 minutes. Add 6 cups broth, then chopped fresh asparagus or frozen asparagus. Bring to boil. Reduce heat; cook until tender, about 10 minutes for fresh or 20 minutes for frozen. Cool slightly.

Working in batches, puree soup in blender. Return to pot; thin with more broth if desired. Season to taste with salt and pepper. *(Can be made 1 day ahead. Cover; chill. Rewarm before serving.)* If using fresh asparagus, add reserved tips and simmer until tips are tender, about 5 minutes.

Serve with a drizzle of sour cream.

10 SERVINGS

The Emerging Immersion Blender

Just as the food processor revolutionized food preparation some two decades ago, so today is the immersion blender bringing new ease to the making of shakes, sauces and pureed soups. As its name may suggest, this long, stick-shaped blender does almost everything a regular blender can do, but portably. One end of the blender, which features a removable blade, is immersed directly into the container of food, making a milk shake in its glass or pureeing a hot soup right in its pot at the touch of a button.

The latest generation of immersion blenders includes several versatile models. Some are powerful enough to crush ice. Others include special attachments such as mini food processors and whisks for whipping cream. Still others are cordless, featuring rechargeable batteries that not only do away with potentially awkward cords but also make it easy to use the blenders where electrical outlets may not be close at hand—poolside, for example, to blend frosty drinks.

Watermelon Lemonade

This drink is sweet, pretty and refreshing. Make a kid-friendly version by omitting the gin. Most grenadine, a pomegranate syrup, is nonalcoholic; check the bottle to be sure one way or the other.

7 cups 2-inch pieces peeled seeded watermelon (from about 4 pounds)
1 cup Simple Syrup (see recipe opposite)
1 cup fresh lemon juice
3 tablespoons grenadine
1 cup gin

3 cups ice cubes
 Lemon twists (optional)

Puree watermelon pieces in processor. Strain watermelon puree into large pitcher, pressing on solids in strainer to extract as much juice as possible. Discard any solids in strainer. Add Simple Syrup, lemon juice and grenadine to pitcher; stir to blend. Stir in gin. *(Lemonade can be prepared 6 hours ahead. Refrigerate.)*

Stir 3 cups ice cubes into watermelon lemonade. Pour into tall glasses. Garnish with lemon twists, if desired, and serve.

6 SERVINGS

beverages

Pineapple-Orange Margarita

2^1/$_2$ cups pineapple juice
1^1/$_4$ cups white tequila
1 cup Cointreau or other orange liqueur
1 cup orange juice
^{3}/$_4$ cup fresh lime juice
^{1}/$_2$ cup Simple Syrup (see recipe below)

3 cups ice cubes
Fresh pineapple spears (optional)
Maraschino cherries (optional)

Combine pineapple juice, tequila, Cointreau, orange juice, lime juice and Simple Syrup in large pitcher. *(Can be made 6 hours ahead. Chill.)*

Add 3 cups ice cubes to pitcher and stir to blend well. Pour Margarita into cocktail glasses. Garnish with pineapple spears and maraschino cherries, if desired, and then serve.

8 SERVINGS

Simple Syrup

3 cups water
1^1/$_2$ cups sugar

Stir 3 cups water and sugar in heavy medium saucepan over medium heat until sugar dissolves. Increase heat and boil 2 minutes. Refrigerate until cold, about 3 hours. *(Can be made 1 week ahead. Cover and keep chilled.)*

MAKES ABOUT 3^1/$_3$ CUPS

A Rainbow of Margaritas

Six decades after it was first created, the tequila-based cocktail known as the Margarita is as popular as its origins are obscure. Various accounts credit the mixture of tequila, triple sec and fresh lime juice to bartenders in the northern Mexican towns of Tequila, Taxco, Tijuana or Juarez, any of which could explain the drink's migration into the American Southwest. As for its name, that could be attributed to a woman who first inspired the drink; or it could describe the beverage's bright, sunshiny nature, as *margarita* in Spanish means "daisy."

The Margarita has come a long way from its vague beginnings. Bartenders now flavor the drink with strawberries, raspberries, peaches, pineapples, oranges, kiwi or melon. And people are just as likely to order the drink frozen (or blended) as they are on the rocks, the more traditional style. "Virgin" Margaritas may be made by substituting orange juice for the triple sec and lemon-lime soda for the tequila.

However you make your Margarita, one thing remains true. After 60 years, it is still an ideal accompaniment to spicy foods, from chips and salsa to good barbecue.

Minted Mai Tai

This is one of many variations on the original mai tai, the classic fruit juice and rum concoction. Look for almond syrup in the coffee and tea section of the supermarket.

$1/2$ cup fresh lime juice
$1/2$ cup almond syrup (such as Torani)
$1/2$ cup chopped fresh mint leaves

2 cups pineapple juice
$1^1/2$ cups orange juice
$1^1/2$ cups dark rum
Ice cubes
6 fresh mint sprigs

Stir lime juice, almond syrup and chopped mint leaves in heavy small saucepan over medium heat just until mixture simmers. Cool.

Strain syrup into pitcher. Add pineapple juice, orange juice and rum; stir to blend. Fill 6 tall glasses with ice. Pour juice mixture over. Garnish mai tais with fresh mint sprigs and serve.

6 SERVINGS

Spumante-Vodka Cocktail with Lemon Sorbet

1 pint (2 cups) frozen lemon sorbet
$1^1/2$ cups spumante or Champagne
6 tablespoons vodka
6 tablespoons whipping cream

Spoon frozen sorbet into blender. Add spumante, vodka and whipping cream. Blend until smooth, about 1 minute. Divide among 6 Champagne flutes or wineglasses and serve.

6 SERVINGS

Berry-Vodka Cooler

1   10-ounce package frozen sweetened raspberries in syrup, thawed
1   10-ounce package frozen sweetened strawberries in syrup, thawed
1/4   cup fresh lemon juice
3   cups black cherry juice
2   cups currant-flavored vodka or plain vodka

2   cups sparkling water
3   cups ice cubes
    Fresh mint sprigs (optional)

Prepare the recipe for the Berry-Vodka Cooler without the alcohol, if desired. Push a large fresh strawberry onto the rim of each glass for an edible garnish.

Combine thawed raspberries with syrup, strawberries with syrup and lemon juice in processor. Puree until smooth. Strain liquid into pitcher; discard solids in strainer. Add cherry juice and vodka. Stir well. *(Can be prepared 6 hours ahead. Refrigerate.)*

Stir sparkling water and ice cubes into pitcher. Pour cooler into cocktail glasses. Garnish with mint, if desired, and serve.

6 SERVINGS

Blue Moon Sake Cocktail

    Ice cubes
1/4   cup sake, chilled
1/4   cup peach Stolichnaya vodka
4   teaspoons blue curaçao
2   teaspoons sweet-and-sour mix

Place 2 Martini glasses in freezer. Fill cocktail shaker with ice cubes. Add sake, vodka, blue curaçao and sweet-and-sour mix to cocktail shaker. Shake well; strain into chilled Martini glasses and serve.

2 SERVINGS

Mixed-Berry Daiquiri

1 10-ounce package frozen sweetened raspberries, thawed
1 cup frozen unsweetened boysenberries, thawed
20 ice cubes (about 3 cups)
1 10-ounce package frozen sweetened strawberries, unthawed, cut into
    8 pieces
1 cup light rum
$^{1}/_{3}$ cup fresh lime juice
1 tablespoon powdered sugar
4 fresh whole strawberries
4 lime wedges

Puree raspberries and boysenberries in blender. Strain puree into bowl, pressing on solids with rubber spatula; discard solids. Return puree to blender. Add ice, frozen strawberries, rum, lime juice and sugar; blend until smooth. Pour into 4 Margarita glasses. Garnish daiquiris with fresh strawberries and lime wedges and serve.

4 SERVINGS

Irish Coffee

1 cup chilled whipping cream
   Sugar
2 cups Irish whiskey
8 tablespoons sugar
6 cups freshly brewed strong coffee

Whisk cream in medium bowl just until slightly thickened but still pourable. Dip rims of 8 glass coffee mugs into water, then into sugar. Pour $^{1}/4$ cup whiskey and 1 tablespoon sugar into each mug. Add coffee. Stir to dissolve sugar. Gently spoon cream mixture over coffee and serve.

8 SERVINGS

The Flavors of Bon Appétit 2001

Strawberry-Banana Smoothie

2 cups sliced hulled strawberries (about one 1-pint basket)
$^1/_4$ cup sugar
1 large ripe banana, peeled, sliced
$^1/_2$ cup chopped pitted peeled mango

$^1/_2$ cup chilled plain nonfat yogurt
6 ice cubes
1 teaspoon vanilla extract
Additional strawberries, left whole (optional)

Toss 2 cups strawberries and $^1/_4$ cup sugar in medium bowl to blend. Let stand at room temperature until juices form, about 1 hour. Add banana and mango to strawberry mixture; place in freezer until partially frozen, about 45 minutes.

Combine fruit mixture, plain nonfat yogurt, ice cubes and vanilla extract in blender. Blend until smooth, about 1 minute. Pour smoothie into glasses. Garnish with whole strawberries, if desired, and serve.

2 TO 4 SERVINGS

Serve this healthful and satisfying drink in chilled glasses on a warm day. It would also make a great breakfast on the go.

Gin, Tea and Lemon Fizz

1 cup water
4 teaspoons black tea leaves or 4 tea bags (such as Darjeeling)
1 cup frozen lemonade concentrate, thawed
1 cup gin
2 cups sparkling water
Ice cubes

Bring 1 cup water to boil in small saucepan. Add tea leaves. Remove from heat. Cover and let steep 15 minutes. Chill overnight. Strain tea mixture into pitcher; discard tea leaves. Add lemonade concentrate and gin, then sparkling water to pitcher; stir to blend. Serve over ice.

6 SERVINGS

Texas-Style
Steak on Toast
(page 49)

Main Courses

meats

poultry

seafood

meatless

pasta & pizza

Southwestern Steak Dinner for Four

Green Chili Tamales

Chili-rubbed Rib-eye Steaks
(at right; pictured opposite)

Pico de Gallo
(at right; pictured opposite)

Garlic Mashed Potatoes
with Corn
(page 128; pictured opposite)

Red Chili Onion Rings
(page 137; pictured opposite)

Microbrew Beer

Crème Brûlée

meats

Chili-rubbed Rib-eye Steaks

RED CHILI POWDER
3 dried ancho or pasilla chilies*
3 dried guajillo or pasilla chilies*

STEAKS
$^1/_4$ cup paprika
2 tablespoons coarse salt
$1^1/_2$ tablespoons sugar
4 14- to 16-ounce bone-in rib-eye steaks (about $1^1/_2$ inches thick)

Nonstick vegetable oil spray
Pico de Gallo (see recipe below)

FOR RED CHILI POWDER: Preheat oven to 350°F. Using small sharp knife, cut stems off chilies and discard. Cut chilies open along 1 long side. Discard seeds. Place chilies on baking sheet. Roast chilies until firm and fragrant, about 5 minutes. Cool. Break chilies into small pieces. Finely grind chilies in spice grinder or blender. *(Can be made 2 weeks ahead. Store airtight at room temperature.)*

FOR STEAKS: Mix $^1/_4$ cup chili powder, paprika, salt and sugar in dish. Coat steaks with mixture; transfer to another dish. Cover; chill at least 8 hours.

Spray grill racks with nonstick spray; prepare barbecue (medium heat). Grill steaks to desired doneness, moving and turning to keep chili rub from burning, 20 minutes for medium-rare. Serve with Pico de Gallo.

*Dried chilies are sold at Latin American markets and some supermarkets.

4 SERVINGS

Pico de Gallo

$1^1/_2$ pounds plum tomatoes, seeded, chopped
$^3/_4$ cup chopped onion
$^1/_2$ cup chopped fresh cilantro
3 tablespoons fresh lime juice
3 tablespoons minced seeded jalapeño chilies (about 2 medium)
1 garlic clove, minced

Mix all ingredients in medium bowl. Season to taste with salt and pepper. *(Can be made 4 hours ahead. Cover; chill.)*

MAKES ABOUT 3 CUPS

Spicy Vietnamese Beef and Noodle Soup

5 tablespoons peanut oil

3¼ pounds meaty oxtails, patted dry

2 large onions, chopped

1 large carrot, peeled, chopped

3 stalks lemongrass,* chopped

⅔ cup chopped peeled fresh ginger

8 garlic cloves, chopped

7 whole star anise (star-shaped spice)*

1 tablespoon black peppercorns

12 cups water

7 cups canned beef broth (about four 14½-ounce cans)

3 tablespoons fish sauce (nam pla)*

1 12-ounce package fresh udon noodles (refrigerated Japanese wheat
    noodles)* or fresh linguine

1 tablespoon oriental sesame oil

3 cups bean sprouts

6 radishes, thinly sliced

4 green onions, thinly sliced

4 serrano chilies, thinly sliced

6 tablespoons chopped fresh basil

6 tablespoons chopped fresh mint

6 tablespoons chopped fresh cilantro

Lime wedges

Additional fish sauce (nam pla)

Heat peanut oil in heavy large pot over medium-high heat. Sprinkle oxtails with salt and pepper. Add oxtails to pot and brown on all sides, about 20 minutes. Transfer oxtails to large bowl. Add onions and next 6 ingredients to same pot. Sauté until vegetables are tender, about 8 minutes. Return oxtails to pot. Add 12 cups water, beef broth and 3 tablespoons fish sauce. Cover and simmer gently until oxtails are very tender, about 3 hours.

Using tongs, transfer oxtails to large bowl. Strain broth into another large pot; discard solids. Remove meat from oxtails; discard bones. Add meat to broth. Refrigerate overnight. Spoon solid fat off top of soup.

Cook noodles in large pot of boiling salted water until tender. Drain; rinse under cold water. Return to pot. Toss with sesame oil. Bring soup to boil. Divide noodles, sprouts and next 6 ingredients among 6 bowls. Ladle soup into bowls. Serve with lime wedges and more fish sauce.

Available at Asian markets and some supermarkets.

6 SERVINGS

Pan-seared Steaks with Goat Cheese, Caper and Tomato Butter

2   ounces soft fresh goat cheese (such as Montrachet), room temperature

2   tablespoons butter, room temperature

2   tablespoons minced drained oil-packed sun-dried tomatoes

1   tablespoon drained capers

2   boneless rib-eye steaks (each about 12 ounces and $1^1/_4$ inches thick)

Using electric mixer, beat cheese and butter in medium bowl until fluffy. Stir in tomatoes and capers. Season with salt and pepper. Spoon butter onto sheet of plastic wrap, forming 3-inch-long log. Wrap and refrigerate until firm. *(Can be made 2 days ahead. Keep refrigerated.)*

Pat steaks dry. Heat large nonstick skillet over high heat. Sprinkle steaks with salt and pepper. Add steaks to skillet and cook 5 minutes per side for medium-rare. Transfer to cutting board. Tent with foil; let stand 5 minutes.

Cut steaks across grain into $^1/_2$-inch-thick slices. Sprinkle with salt and pepper. Divide slices among plates. Using hot sharp knife, cut butter log into 4 rounds. Place 1 butter round atop each serving.

4 SERVINGS

Even Better Than Butter

One of the latest restaurant trends for embellishing grilled seafood, poultry or steaks harks back to a classic French preparation, *beurre composé,* or compound butter. Made by combining butter with lively flavorings, compound butter is formed into pats that are placed atop food at the moment of service, melting to form an instant sauce.

To make a compound butter, start with room-temperature unsalted butter. Using a wooden spoon or electric hand mixer, whip it in a mixing bowl until light. Next, beat in a favorite minced seasoning—fresh herbs, lightly sautéed garlic, sun-dried tomatoes, capers or jalapeños, to name a few. Cheese may also be added: Try goat cheese, crumbled blue cheese or grated Parmesan. Season the butter to taste with salt and pepper, then wrap it loosely in plastic, rolling to form a log. Wrap tightly and refrigerate or freeze until firm.

Compound butters keep up to two days in the refrigerator or one month in the freezer. Thaw in the refrigerator, if frozen, and use chilled. Besides adding flavor to grilled foods, compound butters also make a great addition to steamed vegetables, pasta or mashed potatoes.

Barbecued Cheddar Burgers

$3^{1}/_{2}$ pounds lean ground beef
 $^{1}/_{2}$ cup purchased barbecue sauce
  1 teaspoon garlic powder
  1 teaspoon salt
  1 teaspoon ground black pepper

  1 cup grated cheddar cheese
 12 sesame-seed hamburger buns, lightly toasted
     Lettuce leaves
     Sliced tomatoes

Mix first 4 ingredients in large bowl until blended. Mix in pepper. Shape meat mixture into 10 patties. *(Can be prepared 8 hours ahead. Cover with plastic wrap and refrigerate.)*

Prepare barbecue (medium-high heat). Grill patties to desired doneness, topping with cheese for last minute of cooking, about 5 minutes per side for medium-rare. Place burgers on bottom halves of buns. Top with lettuce, tomatoes and upper halves of buns.

MAKES 10

Stewed Beef with Creamy Polenta

1	3^1/$_4$-pound boneless beef chuck roast (about 2 inches thick), trimmed
^{1}/$_2$	cup matchstick-size strips pancetta or bacon
1	750-ml bottle dry red wine
2	tablespoons olive oil
1	large onion, chopped
2	carrots, peeled, cut into ^{1}/$_2$-inch-thick rounds
2	celery stalks, cut into ^{1}/$_2$-inch-thick pieces
2	bay leaves
1	tablespoon whole juniper berries*
^{1}/$_2$	ounce dried porcini mushrooms,** rinsed to remove grit
1	teaspoon whole black peppercorns
2	whole cloves
	Basic Polenta (see recipe below)

In this typical Northern Italian entrée, polenta is topped with a rich and meaty *ragù*. Begin preparing the dish one day before serving.

Using small knife, cut 1-inch-deep slits all over beef. Fill each with pancetta strip. Place in large bowl; pour wine over. Cover; chill overnight.

Drain wine from beef; reserve wine. Pat beef dry. Heat oil in large pot over high heat. Add beef; cook until brown on both sides, 10 minutes. Add wine, onion and next 7 ingredients. Bring to boil. Reduce heat to medium-low. Cover; cook until beef is very tender, turning occasionally, 2 hours 45 minutes.

Using tongs, transfer beef to platter. Tent with foil to keep warm. Discard bay leaves. Working in batches, coarsely puree wine mixture in blender. Return to pot and bring to simmer. Season with salt and pepper.

Spoon polenta into large bowl. Cut beef into ^{1}/$_2$-inch-thick slices. Arrange beef atop polenta. Spoon sauce over beef and serve.

Available in the spice section of most supermarkets nationwide.
**Available at Italian markets and many supermarkets nationwide.*

8 SERVINGS

Basic Polenta

8	cups water
2	teaspoons salt
2	cups polenta (coarse cornmeal)

Combine 8 cups water and salt in large saucepan. Bring to boil. Gradually add polenta, whisking until smooth. Reduce heat to low. Cover and cook until polenta is thick and creamy, stirring frequently, 30 minutes.

8 SERVINGS

Stocking the Pantry, Japanese Style

Thanks to the ever-growing popularity of Japanese food, special ingredients called for in this style of cooking can now be found not only in Asian markets but also in some natural foods stores and in the Asian foods section of some supermarkets. Use the following descriptions to help you find these items.

- Daikon: This large Japanese white radish has sweet but slightly peppery flesh. It can be braised or steamed, but is most often grated raw and served as a condiment.
- Dried Bonito Shavings: Used as a flavoring for broths, these flakes of steamed, smoked and dried bonito fillet (a type of tuna) are sold in cellophane packages labeled *katsuo-bushi*.
- Dried Kelp: Another ingredient used to flavor broths, this form of seaweed is called *konbu* or *dashi-konbu* and is sold in flat sheets. Choose dark-green blades that are about four inches wide.
- Japanese Plum Wine: This dessert wine, actually made from unripe *ume* apricots, has a delicately sweet fruit flavor. You'll find it in liquor stores or the liquor department of some supermarkets. If unavailable, substitute cream Sherry.
- *Mirin*: A sweet, slightly syrupy rice wine, mirin is found in the Asian foods section or the supermarket's liquor department.

Ginger Beef Tataki with Lemon-Soy Dipping Sauce

2 tablespoons vegetable oil
1 2-pound piece beef tenderloin, trimmed

6 tablespoons soy sauce
$^1/_4$ cup mirin (sweet Japanese rice wine)*
2 green onions, very thinly sliced
2 tablespoons (packed) golden brown sugar
2 tablespoons fresh lemon juice
2 tablespoons minced peeled fresh ginger
2 large garlic cloves, flattened

6 tablespoons finely grated peeled daikon (Japanese white radish)*
6 tablespoons finely grated peeled fresh ginger
4 green onions, very finely chopped
2 lemons, cut into wedges
Shiso (beefsteak plant leaves)* or watercress
Lemon-Soy Dipping Sauce (see recipe opposite)

Preheat oven to 400°F. Rub 1 tablespoon oil over beef. Sprinkle beef with salt and pepper. Heat remaining 1 tablespoon oil in heavy large skillet over medium-high heat. Add beef to skillet and cook until brown, turning often, about 5 minutes.

Transfer beef to roasting pan. Roast beef in oven until thermometer inserted into center registers 130°F for medium-rare, about 35 minutes. Cool.

Combine soy sauce and next 6 ingredients in large resealable plastic bag. Add beef to marinade. Seal bag and refrigerate until beef is cold, turning in marinade occasionally, at least 4 hours and up to 1 day.

Discard marinade. Cut beef into $^1/_4$-inch-thick slices. Cover and let stand at room temperature 30 minutes. Arrange beef on plates. Spoon small mounds of daikon, ginger and chopped green onions onto plates. Garnish with lemon wedges and shiso. Serve beef with individual bowls of Lemon-Soy Dipping Sauce.

Available at Japanese markets and in the Asian foods section of some supermarkets.

6 SERVINGS

The Flavors of Bon Appétit 2001

Lemon-Soy Dipping Sauce

$1/2$ cup soy sauce

$1/4$ cup fresh lemon juice

2 tablespoons mirin (sweet Japanese rice wine)*

2 tablespoons water

1 tablespoon dried bonito shavings (katsuo-bushi)*

Combine all ingredients in small bowl. Let stand 30 minutes. Strain sauce through fine strainer; discard bonito shavings.

Available at Japanese markets and in some supermarkets.

MAKES ABOUT 1 CUP

Texas-Style Steak on Toast

1 teaspoon chili powder

$1/2$ teaspoon dark brown sugar

1 $1^1/_2$-pound top sirloin steak (about 1 inch thick), trimmed

1 cup coarsely chopped seeded tomatoes

$1/2$ cup pitted Kalamata olives or other brine-cured black olives

5 tablespoons plus 2 teaspoons extra-virgin olive oil

2 teaspoons red wine vinegar

2 tablespoons minced red onion

8 1-inch-thick slices French bread

2 bunches watercress, thick stems trimmed

Mix chili powder and brown sugar in small bowl to blend. Rub mixture over steak. Sprinkle with salt and pepper.

Combine tomatoes, olives, 2 tablespoons oil and vinegar in processor. Using on/off turns, blend just until olives are coarsely chopped. Transfer to bowl. Stir in onion. Season relish with salt and pepper.

Heat 2 teaspoons oil in large skillet over medium-high heat. Add steak and cook to desired doneness, 3 minutes per side for medium-rare. Transfer to plate. Let stand 5 minutes. Wipe out skillet. Brush 1 side of all bread with 3 tablespoons oil. Heat skillet over medium heat. Add bread, oiled side down; cook until golden, about 2 minutes per side.

Cut steak across grain into $1/_4$-inch-thick slices. Spread relish generously over oiled side of 4 toasts. Top with watercress, then steak slices. Top with a bit more relish, then remaining toasts.

4 SERVINGS

- Red Miso: This dark, brick-colored fermented soybean paste is used to flavor soups and stews. Look for it in the refrigerated section; it's also called barley miso, brown miso or, in Japanese, *aka-miso*.
- *Shiso:* The small dark-green or red leaves of the beefsteak plant, a member of the mint family, have jagged edges and a fresh, minty flavor. They are popular as a flavoring for sushi, as tempura or as a garnish.
- Shredded Red Pickled Ginger: This red-tinted ginger, called *beni shoga*, is pickled and usually sold in jars for use as a garnish.
- Sweet White Miso: This light-colored fermented soybean paste is found in the refrigerated section and is often labeled *shiro-miso*. Yellow miso *(chumiso)*, a mellow, light-brown miso, is more widely available and may be substituted. Use it in soups and salad dressings.
- Tofu: Made from soy milk, this pale beige bean curd is found in the refrigerated section, shaped into a brick and packed in liquid. A rich source of protein, tofu may be simmered, braised, fried or grilled.

Grilled Tri-Tip Roast with Tequila Marinade and Cherry Tomato Relish

$^1/_2$ cup fresh lime juice

$^1/_2$ cup chopped fresh cilantro

$^1/_2$ cup olive oil

$^1/_3$ cup soy sauce

$^1/_4$ cup tequila

7 garlic cloves, finely chopped

2 teaspoons grated lime peel

2 teaspoons ground cumin

2 teaspoons dried oregano

1 teaspoon ground black pepper

2 2-pound beef loin tri-tip roasts, trimmed

Cherry Tomato Relish (see recipe below)

Whisk first 10 ingredients in medium bowl to blend. Using small sharp knife, pierce meat all over. Place meat in large resealable plastic bag; add marinade. Seal bag. Refrigerate at least 2 hours or overnight, turning plastic bag occasionally.

Prepare barbecue (medium-high heat). Discard marinade. Grill meat to desired doneness, 10 minutes per side for medium-rare. Transfer to cutting board. Tent with foil; let stand 10 minutes. Cut diagonally across grain. Serve with Cherry Tomato Relish.

8 SERVINGS

Cherry Tomato Relish

$^1/_4$ cup balsamic vinegar

4 teaspoons chopped fresh oregano

$^3/_4$ cup olive oil

$^2/_3$ cup drained canned diced mild green chilies

4 green onions, finely chopped

4 cups halved cherry tomatoes

Whisk vinegar and oregano in medium bowl to blend. Gradually whisk in oil. Mix in green chilies and green onions. *(Can be made 6 hours ahead. Cover; chill.)* Add tomatoes; toss to coat. Season with salt and pepper.

8 SERVINGS

Summer Celebration Dinner for Eight

Guacamole with Tomatoes, Cilantro and Jalapeños
(page 24)

Tortilla Chips

Grilled Tri-Tip Roast with Tequila Marinade and Cherry Tomato Relish
(at left; pictured opposite)

Coleslaw

Potato Salad with Chilies and Corn
(page 204)

Mexican Beer with Lime Wedges

Spiced Peach Sundaes
(page 215)

Veal Burgers Stuffed with Mozzarella Cheese

This sophisticated take on cheese-burgers goes well with the usual fries or chips. Add tomato slices and lettuce to the burgers, if you like.

෴

1 cup shredded mozzarella cheese
$^1/_4$ cup finely chopped green onions
1$^1/_4$ pounds ground veal
2 teaspoons Worcestershire sauce
1 teaspoon salt
$^3/_4$ teaspoon ground black pepper

$^1/_2$ cup mayonnaise
2 teaspoons coarse-grained mustard
1 teaspoon grated lemon peel
$^1/_2$ teaspoon dried rubbed sage

4 4-inch-diameter portobello mushrooms, stemmed
6 tablespoons olive oil
2 garlic cloves, minced

4 large sesame-seed buns, split, toasted

Mix cheese and green onions in medium bowl. Gently mix ground veal, Worcestershire sauce, salt and pepper in large bowl. Divide veal mixture into 4 equal portions. Divide 1 portion in half; form two $^3/_8$-inch-thick patties. Place $^1/_4$ cup cheese mixture atop 1 patty; top with second patty. Seal at edges to enclose cheese mixture. Repeat with remaining 3 portions.

Mix next 4 ingredients in small bowl. *(Patties and mayonnaise mixture can be made 2 hours ahead. Cover separately and refrigerate.)*

Preheat oven to 400°F. Place portobello mushrooms on rimmed baking sheet. Combine 4 tablespoons olive oil and garlic. Brush over both sides of mushrooms. Sprinkle with salt and pepper. Roast mushrooms until tender, turning once, about 20 minutes.

Heat 2 tablespoons oil in heavy large skillet over medium-high heat. Add burgers and cook until cheese melts, about 5 minutes per side.

Spread mayonnaise mixture over buns. Place burgers on bottom halves. Top with mushrooms, then with bun tops, and serve.

4 SERVINGS

Veal with Tomato-Basil Sauce

1 pound veal cutlets (about 8 small)
  All purpose flour
6 tablespoons (about) olive oil
4 large garlic cloves, chopped
2 14$^1/_2$- to 15-ounce cans diced tomatoes in juice
$^1/_4$ cup (packed) chopped fresh basil
2 tablespoons chopped Italian parsley
1 teaspoon dried oregano
$^1/_2$ teaspoon dried crushed red pepper
8 ounces mozzarella cheese, thinly sliced

Sprinkle veal with salt and pepper; dust with flour. Heat 4 tablespoons oil in heavy large skillet over medium-high heat. Working in batches, add veal to skillet and sauté until brown, 2 minutes per side. Transfer to plate. Add remaining 2 tablespoons oil to same skillet. Add garlic and sauté until fragrant, 30 seconds. Add tomatoes with juices, basil, parsley, oregano and dried red pepper. Bring sauce to boil. Reduce heat to medium-low; simmer until flavors blend and sauce thickens, scraping up browned bits, 8 minutes. Season with salt and pepper. Arrange cutlets atop sauce. Top each with cheese. Cover; simmer until veal is tender and cheese melts, 5 minutes.

4 SERVINGS

Veal Sauté with Merlot Pan Sauce

10 ounces veal cutlets
4 teaspoons minced fresh sage
3 tablespoons butter
1 large shallot, chopped
$^1/_2$ cup Merlot or other dry red wine

Using rolling pin, pound veal between sheets of waxed paper to $^1/_4$-inch thickness. Sprinkle veal with 3 teaspoons sage, salt and pepper. Melt 2 tablespoons butter in heavy large skillet over medium-high heat. Add veal and cook to desired doneness, about 3 minutes per side for medium. Transfer to plates. Add shallot to skillet; stir 30 seconds. Add wine and 1 tablespoon butter. Boil sauce until reduced almost to glaze, scraping up any browned bits, 2 minutes. Spoon sauce over veal; sprinkle with 1 teaspoon sage.

2 SERVINGS

Easy Italian Dinner
for Four

Mixed Baby Greens with
  Balsamic Vinaigrette,
  Grated Parmesan and
  Toasted Pine Nuts

Veal with Tomato-Basil Sauce
  (at left)

Angel Hair Pasta Tossed with
  Olive Oil

Crusty Bread

Chianti

Biscotti and Ice Cream

Veal Shoulder with Porcini Mushrooms, Garlic and Rosemary

1	$^3/_4$-ounce package dried porcini mushrooms
8	large garlic cloves
1	tablespoon chopped fresh rosemary
1	tablespoon fresh thyme leaves
1	teaspoon kosher salt
$^1/_2$	teaspoon ground black pepper
1	5-pound veal shoulder clod roast, tied to hold shape
$^1/_4$	cup olive oil
2	pounds meaty veal neck bones
4	cups canned low-salt chicken broth
$^1/_2$	cup dry red wine
$^1/_2$	cup drained chopped canned tomatoes
3	tablespoons tomato paste
1	tablespoon balsamic vinegar

Preheat oven to 350°F. Grind mushrooms to powder in coffee or spice mill. Coarsely chop garlic, rosemary, thyme, salt and pepper in processor. Set aside 1 tablespoon garlic mixture; press remainder, $^1/_2$ teaspoon at a time, into center of veal through openings of string (or poke holes in veal and push garlic mixture in). Coat outside of veal with mushroom powder.

Heat oil in heavy large pot over medium-high heat. Add bones and brown well, about 8 minutes. Transfer bones to bowl. Add veal to pot. Brown on all sides, about 5 minutes. Add reserved 1 tablespoon garlic mixture and any remaining mushroom powder to pot around veal and stir 1 minute. Arrange bones around veal. Add broth, wine, tomatoes, tomato paste and vinegar. Bring to boil. Cover; place in oven and roast until veal is tender, turning veal every 30 minutes, about 2 hours.

Cool veal uncovered 1 hour. Discard bones. Refrigerate until cold, then cover and keep refrigerated 1 day.

Scrape off fat from surface of sauce. Transfer veal to work surface, scraping any sauce back into pot. Remove strings. Cut veal crosswise into scant $^1/_2$-inch-thick slices. Overlap slices in large baking dish. Boil sauce until reduced to $3^1/_2$ cups, about 20 minutes. Season to taste with salt and pepper. Spoon sauce over veal. *(Can be prepared 2 days ahead. Cover with foil and refrigerate.)*

Preheat oven to 350°F. Bake veal covered until heated, about 35 minutes.

8 SERVINGS

Rosemary and Garlic Lamb Chops

5	garlic cloves
3	tablespoons extra-virgin olive oil
2^1/$_2$	teaspoons chopped fresh rosemary
2	teaspoons salt
1	teaspoon freshly ground black pepper
12	meaty lamb rib chops (about 2^1/$_2$ ounces each)

Combine first 5 ingredients in processor; blend until garlic is finely chopped. Coat chops with garlic mixture. Arrange chops in single layer on baking sheet. *(Can be made 8 hours ahead. Cover; chill.)*

Preheat broiler. Watching closely, broil lamb 4 to 5 inches from heat source until cooked to desired doneness, about 3 minutes per side for medium-rare. Transfer 3 chops to each plate and serve.

4 SERVINGS

Grilled Lamb Kebabs with Cumin and Cinnamon

^{1}/$_4$	cup olive oil
1	teaspoon ground cumin
1	teaspoon ground black pepper
^{3}/$_4$	teaspoon salt
^{1}/$_2$	teaspoon ground cinnamon
1	3^1/$_2$-pound sirloin half leg of lamb, bone removed, fat trimmed, meat cut into 1^1/$_4$- to 1^1/$_2$-inch pieces
6	12-inch metal skewers

Whisk first 5 ingredients in 13x9x2-inch glass baking dish. Add lamb to dish and toss to coat with oil mixture. Let marinate at room temperature 1 hour or refrigerate 1^1/$_2$ to 4 hours, tossing occasionally.

Prepare barbecue (medium heat) or preheat broiler. Thread marinated lamb pieces onto skewers, dividing equally. Grill or broil lamb to desired doneness, turning occasionally, about 6 minutes for medium-rare.

6 SERVINGS

City-Style Dinner for Four

Artichokes with Romano,
Cracked Pepper and Olive Oil
(page 22)

Rosemary and Garlic
Lamb Chops
(at left; pictured opposite)

Saffron Couscous with
Fresh Peas and Chives
(page 135; pictured opposite)

Steamed Baby Carrots

Cabernet Sauvignon

Rhubarb Napoleons
(page 165; pictured opposite)

Spice-crusted Rack of Lamb

    2   tablespoons whole coriander seeds
    4   teaspoons black peppercorns
    2   teaspoons cumin seeds
   12   whole cloves
    1   teaspoon ground turmeric
  3/4   teaspoon cardamom seeds (from whole green pods)

    3   tablespoons vegetable oil
    2   pounds meaty lamb neck bones
    2   celery stalks, chopped
    1   cup chopped onion
    8   large garlic cloves, chopped
    2   tablespoons chopped peeled fresh ginger
    3   small bay leaves, crumbled
    2   large plum tomatoes, chopped
    5   cups canned low-salt chicken broth
  1/2   cup dry white wine
  1/4   cup chopped fresh mint

    3   1 1/4-pound lamb racks

Blend all spices to powder in grinder. Transfer spice rub to bowl.

Heat oil in large pot over medium-high heat. Add bones; sauté until brown, about 10 minutes. Add celery, onion, garlic, ginger and bay leaves. Reduce heat to medium; sauté until celery is tender, about 5 minutes. Mix in tomatoes and 2 tablespoons spice rub; stir 2 minutes. Add broth, wine and mint. Bring to boil. Reduce heat to medium-low; cover and simmer 1 1/2 hours. Strain into medium saucepan, pressing hard on solids in sieve. Spoon fat off top of broth; reserve fat for use with lamb. Boil broth until reduced to 1 1/2 cups, about 25 minutes. Season sauce with salt and pepper.

Brush each lamb rack with reserved lamb fat. Sprinkle each with salt and pepper; rub each with 1 tablespoon spice rub. Place on rimmed baking sheet. Let stand at room temperature 2 hours. *(Sauce and lamb can be made 1 day ahead. Cover separately; chill. Bring to room temperature before continuing.)*

Preheat oven to 400°F. Heat large skillet over high heat. Sear 1 lamb rack on all sides until brown, about 8 minutes. Return to baking sheet. Repeat with remaining lamb racks. Roast lamb until thermometer inserted into center registers 125°F for rare, about 25 minutes.

Rewarm sauce. Cut lamb into chops. Spoon sauce over lamb.

6 SERVINGS

Spicy Lamb and Chorizo Chili

2¹/₄ cups canned low-salt chicken broth

3 ounces dried ancho chilies* (about 5 large), stemmed, seeded,
    torn into pieces

1 teaspoon cayenne pepper

2 1-pound rolls beef or pork chorizo, casings removed

2 cups coarsely chopped red onions

12 large garlic cloves, chopped

1 tablespoon dried leaf oregano

1 tablespoon ground cumin

3¹/₄ pounds o-bone (round-bone) lamb shoulder chops, boned,
    cut into ³/₄-inch cubes

2 15-ounce cans golden hominy or pinto beans, rinsed, drained

Combine first 3 ingredients in heavy medium saucepan. Cover and simmer over medium heat until chilies soften, about 12 minutes. Working in batches, puree chili mixture in blender.

Stir chorizo in heavy large pot over medium-high heat until drippings come to simmer, breaking up meat with spoon. Transfer to fine strainer set over bowl. Let chorizo drain 10 minutes.

Return ¹/₄ cup chorizo drippings to same pot and heat over medium-high heat (discard remaining drippings). Add onions, garlic, oregano and cumin. Sauté until onions begin to soften, about 5 minutes. Sprinkle lamb with salt and pepper; add to pot. Sauté until lamb is no longer pink outside, about 10 minutes. Add chili puree and drained chorizo. Bring chili to boil, stirring occasionally. Reduce heat to medium-low, cover and simmer 1 hour. Add hominy. Simmer uncovered until lamb is tender and liquid thickens, stirring occasionally, about 15 minutes. Season with salt and pepper. (Can be made 3 days ahead. Chill uncovered until cold, then cover and keep chilled. Rewarm before serving.)

*Available at Latin American markets and some supermarkets.

6 TO 8 SERVINGS

Roast Leg of Lamb with Lemon-Coriander Crust

Begin preparing the lamb the day before you plan to serve it; marinating the lamb overnight infuses it with flavor. Use a food processor to make the fresh breadcrumbs.

2 small lemons (with peel), cut into $^1/_4$-inch pieces
$^1/_4$ cup sugar
$^1/_4$ cup water

$^1/_2$ cup (1 stick) butter, room temperature
6 tablespoons soft breadcrumbs (made from French bread)
3 tablespoons ground coriander

1 large lemon, thinly sliced
10 garlic cloves, unpeeled, halved lengthwise
6 fresh thyme sprigs
4 fresh rosemary sprigs
1 tablespoon coriander seeds
1 $7^1/_2$-pound bone-in leg of lamb
2 cups extra-virgin olive oil

$^1/_4$ cup water (if needed)

$^1/_2$ cup dry white wine
2 cups chicken stock or canned low-salt chicken broth

Stir first 3 ingredients in small saucepan over low heat until sugar dissolves. Simmer until lemons are very tender and mixture is reduced to $^1/_3$ cup, stirring occasionally, about 45 minutes. Cool lemon marmalade.

Mix $2^1/_2$ tablespoons lemon marmalade (reserve remainder for another use), butter, breadcrumbs and ground coriander in medium bowl. Season to taste with salt and pepper. Spoon butter mixture onto plastic wrap and shape into 6x1$^1/_2$ x 1$^1/_2$-inch rectangle. Wrap in plastic and refrigerate until very firm, at least 2 hours or overnight. Slice butter into $^1/_4$-inch-thick slices; wrap and refrigerate until ready to use. *(Lemon-coriander butter can be made 2 days ahead. Keep refrigerated.)*

Scatter half of lemon slices and half each of garlic, thyme, rosemary and coriander seeds in bottom of large roasting pan. Place lamb atop mixture in pan. Pour olive oil over lamb. Top with remaining lemon slices, garlic, thyme, rosemary and coriander seeds. Cover and refrigerate overnight, turning lamb over twice.

Preheat oven to 425°F. Scrape herbs off lamb and back into roasting pan; transfer lamb to baking sheet. Pour marinade through strainer; discard oil. Spread strained lemon-herb mixture on bottom of same roasting pan. Place lamb atop lemon-herb mixture. Roast lamb until thermometer inserted into thickest part registers 135°F for medium-rare, basting with pan juices every 10 minutes and adding ¼ cup water to pan if drippings appear ready to burn, about 1 hour 15 minutes.

Increase oven temperature to 500°F. Transfer lamb to platter. Strain pan juices into bowl. Degrease pan juices. Set roasting pan over medium-high heat. Add wine to pan and bring to boil, scraping up browned bits. Boil until almost all liquid evaporates, about 3 minutes. Add degreased juices and stock to pan and boil until reduced to 1½ cups, about 5 minutes. Remove sauce from heat. Add 1½ tablespoons lemon-coriander butter; whisk sauce to melt.

Slice remaining lemon-coriander butter and place slices side by side atop lamb, covering top. Roast until crust browns, about 10 minutes. Transfer lamb to platter. Using back of spoon, spread crust to cover any open spaces, if desired. Slice lamb and serve with sauce.

8 SERVINGS

Mediterranean Supper for Eight

Mixed Baby Greens with Fresh Mozzarella, Cherry Tomatoes and Balsamic Vinaigrette

Roast Leg of Lamb with Lemon-Coriander Crust
(opposite; pictured at left)

Roast Summer Vegetables

Syrah

Raspberry-Crème Fraîche Tart
(page 212)

Braised Lamb Shanks with
Winter Squash and Red Chard

Browning the lamb creates a crust that adds flavor and color to the meat and sauce. Use tongs (not a fork) to turn the lamb to keep the meat from being pierced and losing juices.

Because the lamb is braised uncovered, the liquid will slowly evaporate, concentrating the flavors. It is necessary to turn the lamb frequently because the exposed surfaces of the meat will continue to brown.

LAMB AND SQUASH

4	$^3/_4$- to 1-pound lamb shanks
2	tablespoons vegetable oil
4	tablespoons ($^1/_2$ stick) butter
1$^1/_2$	cups chopped onions
1	cup chopped carrots
1	cup chopped parsnips
4	large fresh thyme sprigs
2	whole garlic heads, unpeeled, cut horizontally in half
1	cup dry red wine
5	cups chicken stock or canned low-salt chicken broth
1	large orange, peel and pith cut away, orange quartered
2	whole cinnamon sticks
2	teaspoons fennel seeds, crushed
1	1$^3/_4$-pound butternut squash, quartered lengthwise, seeded
$^1/_2$	teaspoon (scant) ground nutmeg
1	fresh medium fennel bulb, trimmed, sliced (about 2 cups)
2	teaspoons grated orange peel

CHARD

2	bunches red Swiss chard
2	tablespoons ($^1/_4$ stick) butter

FOR LAMB AND SQUASH: Preheat oven to 375°F. Sprinkle lamb on all sides with salt and pepper. Heat oil in heavy large ovenproof pot over high heat. Add lamb; cook until brown, turning occasionally, about 10 minutes. Transfer to plate. Add 1 tablespoon butter to drippings in pot. Add onions, carrots, parsnips, thyme and garlic. Sauté until vegetables soften and begin to brown, about 8 minutes. Add wine; boil until reduced almost to glaze, about 4 minutes. Return lamb to pot, arranging in single layer. Add chicken stock, orange, cinnamon sticks and 1 teaspoon fennel seeds; bring to boil. Place pot in oven. Braise lamb uncovered until tender, turning and basting often, about 2 hours 15 minutes.

Meanwhile, rub cut sides of squash with 1 tablespoon butter; sprinkle with salt and pepper. Arrange squash, skin side down, on baking sheet. Roast on sheet alongside lamb until tender, about 1 hour 15 minutes. Scrape squash from skins into bowl; add nutmeg and remaining 2 tablespoons butter. Mash with fork until almost smooth; season with salt and pepper.

To finish the sauce, first pour the braising liquid through a sieve set over a large bowl, then discard the chopped vegetables.

Once strained, the sauce should simmer until it is thick enough to coat a spatula.

Transfer lamb to plate. Strain braising liquid into bowl; spoon off fat, if desired. Return liquid to pot. Add fresh fennel, orange peel and remaining 1 teaspoon fennel seeds. Simmer until fennel is tender and sauce is thick enough to coat spoon, about 15 minutes. Return lamb to sauce.

Rewarm lamb shanks, covered, over medium-low heat, 15 minutes. Rewarm squash in saucepan over low heat, stirring often, 10 minutes.

MEANWHILE, PREPARE CHARD: While lamb and squash heat, cut out center stem from chard leaves; discard stems. Coarsely tear leaves. Melt butter in heavy large skillet over high heat. Add chard and toss until chard wilts, about 4 minutes. Season to taste with salt and pepper.

Divide squash and chard among 4 plates. Arrange lamb atop vegetables; spoon sauce with fennel over and serve.

4 SERVINGS

Coriander Pork Tenderloin with Carrot-Ginger Sauce

    1   pound carrots, peeled, cut into 1-inch pieces
    3   cups water
  $3/4$ teaspoon salt
  $1/3$ cup whipping cream
    1   tablespoon finely grated peeled fresh ginger

  $1/4$ cup whole coriander seeds
    3   pork tenderloins (about 3 pounds total), trimmed
    2   tablespoons olive oil

Combine carrots, 3 cups water and salt in heavy medium saucepan. Bring to boil. Reduce heat to low. Cover and cook until carrots are very tender, about 30 minutes. Drain; reserve cooking liquid. Transfer carrots to processor. Puree until smooth. Add cream and ginger and process to blend. Transfer puree to heavy small saucepan. Add enough reserved cooking liquid to puree to form consistency of thick sauce. Season sauce to taste with salt and pepper. *(Can be prepared 1 day ahead. Cover and refrigerate. Rewarm before serving.)*

Coarsely grind coriander seeds in spice grinder or blender. Sprinkle pork with salt and pepper. Press coriander onto pork, coating completely. Heat 1 tablespoon oil in each of 2 heavy large nonstick skillets over medium-high heat. Add 1 pork tenderloin to 1 skillet and 2 pork tenderloins to second skillet. Brown pork on all sides and cook until thermometer inserted into center registers 155°F, about 25 minutes.

Transfer pork to cutting board. Let rest 5 minutes. Cut pork into 1-inch-thick slices. Spoon sauce onto plates. Top with pork and serve.

6 SERVINGS

Sophisticated Far East Dinner for Six

Oysters on the Half Shell

Coriander Pork Tenderloin with
  Carrot-Ginger Sauce
    (at left; pictured opposite)

Jasmine Rice Timbales with
  Sesame Seeds
    (page 129; pictured opposite)

Steamed Snow Peas and
  Baby Corn

Dry Gewürztraminer

Melon and Pineapple Salad with
  Toasted Coconut

Sweet-and-Smoky Baby Back Ribs with Bourbon Barbecue Sauce

6   baby back pork rib racks
1   cup bourbon

3   tablespoons coarse salt
3   tablespoons (packed) dark brown sugar
3   tablespoons paprika
2   tablespoons ground black pepper
1   tablespoon garlic powder
1   teaspoon ground cumin

2   cups hickory wood chips
2   cups beer

Bourbon Barbecue Sauce (see recipe opposite)

Arrange ribs in large roasting pan. Pour bourbon over. Chill 30 minutes, turning ribs often. Pour off and discard bourbon.

Whisk salt and next 5 ingredients in medium bowl. Sprinkle spice mixture on both sides of ribs. Let stand 1 hour.

Place wood chips in medium bowl. Pour beer over; let stand 1 hour.

Place handful of torn newspaper in bottom of charcoal chimney. Top newspaper with 25 charcoal briquettes. Remove upper rack from barbecue. Place chimney on lower grill rack. Light newspaper and let charcoal burn until ash is gray, about 30 minutes.

Open 1 bottom grill vent. Turn out hot charcoal onto 1 side of lower rack. Using metal spatula, spread charcoal to cover approximately 1/3 of rack. Remove 1 cup wood chips from beer and drain (keep remaining chips in beer). Scatter drained chips over coals (avoid using too many wet chips, which may douse the fire). Fill foil loaf pan halfway with water and place opposite coals on lower grill rack.

Place upper grill rack on barbecue. Arrange ribs on upper grill rack above loaf pan. Cover barbecue with lid, positioning top vent directly over ribs. Place stem of candy thermometer through top vent, with gauge on outside and tip near ribs (thermometer should not touch meat or grill rack); leave in place during cooking. Check temperature after 5 minutes. Use top and bottom vents to maintain temperature between 275°F and 325°F, opening vents wider to increase heat and closing to decrease heat. Leave any other vents closed.

Wood Chips, Smoking and Your Grill

Fragrant wood chips such as hickory, apple, pecan and alder can add flavor to foods cooked on the grill. Look for the chips in stores where grills are sold, as well as in specialty foods and kitchenware stores. Soaking the chips in water before use helps them generate smoke. They can be scattered over glowing coals (or placed in a special smoke box for use with a gas grill) just before grilled foods are done, or used as part of a slow, moist smoking process. To convert your grill to a smoker, follow these steps.

- Soak the wood chips in cold water at least 30 minutes.
- Close all but one vent on the bottom of your grill.

After 45 minutes, use technique described above to light 15 briquettes in same charcoal chimney set atop nonflammable surface.

When temperature of barbecue falls below 275°F, use mitts to lift off upper rack with ribs; place rack with ribs on heatproof surface. Using tongs, add hot gray charcoal from chimney to bottom rack. Drain remaining 1 cup wood chips; sprinkle over charcoal. Reposition upper rack on barbecue, placing ribs above loaf pan. Cover with lid. Grill until ribs are very tender and meat pulls away from bones, about 45 minutes, brushing with 3/4 cup Bourbon Barbecue Sauce the last 15 minutes of cooking.

Transfer ribs to platter. Brush with 3/4 cup more barbecue sauce. Serve, passing remaining sauce separately, if desired.

6 SERVINGS

Bourbon Barbecue Sauce

2	cups ketchup
1/2	cup mild-flavored (light) molasses
1/3	cup bourbon
1/4	cup Dijon mustard
3	tablespoons hot pepper sauce
2	tablespoons Worcestershire sauce
2	teaspoons paprika
1	teaspoon garlic powder
1	teaspoon onion powder

Combine all ingredients in heavy large saucepan. Bring to boil over medium heat, stirring occasionally. Reduce heat to medium-low; simmer uncovered until sauce thickens and flavors blend, stirring frequently, about 15 minutes. *(Can be made 1 week ahead. Cover; chill.)*

MAKES ABOUT 2 1/2 CUPS

- Use a charcoal chimney to ignite 25 charcoal briquettes (or an equivalent amount of lump charcoal), setting chimney on a nonflammable surface. Charcoal is ready when just ash-gray in color. Turn out hot charcoal onto one side of lower barbecue rack. Using a long-handled metal spatula, spread charcoal to cover about one-third of rack.

- Drain about one cup of wood chips. Scatter chips over coals (avoid using too many wet chips, which can extinguish the fire).

- Fill a foil loaf pan halfway with water; place on lower rack opposite charcoal. Add boiling water to pan as needed to maintain water level.

- Place meat on upper rack above pan (not above charcoal).

- Cover grill, positioning top vent over meat to draw smoke over it.

- Hang stem of barbecue thermometer through top vent in cover. Use vents to maintain temperature range, opening vents to increase temperature and closing slightly to reduce temperature.

- When temperature drops below specified range (about once an hour), light 15 more charcoal lumps in chimney. Add charcoal to barbecue when ash-gray in color, along with one cup drained wood chips.

- Open barbecue only when necessary (to baste meat, for instance) to minimize loss of heat and smoke.

Skillet Choucroute with Potatoes

Choucroute, which is French for "sauerkraut," makes a complete meal when garnished with sausage and potatoes; this hearty combination is sometimes called choucroute garni.

10 ¹/₂-inch-thick diagonal slices kielbasa sausage (about 8 ounces)
 1 small onion, sliced
1¹/₂ tablespoons chopped fresh thyme or 1 teaspoon dried
 1 cup apple juice or cider
¹/₂ cup canned beef broth
¹/₂ cup drained sauerkraut (from jar or can)
12 ounces red-skinned new potatoes, halved, thinly sliced crosswise

Cook kielbasa in heavy large skillet over medium-high heat until sausage is beginning to brown and some fat is rendered, about 3 minutes. Add onion and thyme. Cover and cook until onion starts to soften, stirring once, about 2 minutes. Add apple juice, broth and sauerkraut. Mix in potatoes. Reduce heat to medium-low. Cover and simmer until potatoes are tender, about 20 minutes. Season with salt and pepper.

2 SERVINGS

Glazed Ham with Pineapple and Cloves

 1 10- to 11-pound fully cooked bone-in ham (rump half)
 1 cup honey
 2 teaspoons dry mustard
¹/₂ teaspoon ground cloves
24 (about) whole cloves

 1 large pineapple, peeled, halved lengthwise, cored, cut crosswise into ¹/₂-inch-thick slices

Preheat oven to 350°F. Place ham on rack in roasting pan. Bake 1¹/₂ hours.

Mix honey, dry mustard and ground cloves in small bowl to blend. Remove ham from oven. Cut off any rind and all but thin layer of fat. Using long knife, score fat in 1-inch-wide diamond pattern. Press 1 whole clove into center of each diamond. Brush ham generously with some of honey glaze. Bake ham 15 minutes.

Using toothpicks, attach pineapple slices to ham. Brush pineapple all over with glaze. Bake 20 minutes longer. Brush again with glaze. Transfer ham to platter. Remove pineapple; arrange alongside ham and serve.

12 SERVINGS

Smoked Ham, Barley and Vegetable Soup

10 cups canned low-salt chicken broth

3 pounds smoked ham hocks

$^3/_4$ pound russet potatoes (about 2 medium), peeled, diced

1 14$^1/_2$-ounce can diced tomatoes in juice

1 medium onion, chopped

2 medium carrots, peeled, chopped

1 cup chopped celery

$^3/_4$ cup pearl barley, rinsed

2 teaspoons dried oregano

8 ounces fresh green beans, trimmed, cut into $^1/_2$-inch pieces

This satisfying soup gets its rich flavor from smoked ham hocks. If you want to prepare it ahead of time, wait to add the fresh green beans until the last minute.

Bring broth and ham hocks to boil in large pot. Cover, reduce heat to medium-low and simmer 15 minutes. Add next 7 ingredients to pot. Bring to boil. Reduce heat to medium-low; simmer soup uncovered until meat and barley are tender, about 1 hour.

Using tongs, remove ham hocks from soup. Cut meat off bones and chop coarsely. Return meat to soup; discard bones. *(Can be prepared 2 days ahead. Refrigerate uncovered until cold, then cover and keep chilled. Bring to simmer before continuing.)* Add green beans; simmer until beans are tender, about 15 minutes. Season with salt and pepper.

8 SERVINGS

Pork Chili Verde Enchiladas

Traditionally, the tortillas for enchiladas are fried in oil until soft. This lighter version calls for wrapping the tortillas in damp paper towels and heating them in the microwave.

2 fresh Anaheim chilies*

1 14¹/₂-ounce can low-salt chicken broth

1¹/₄ cups chopped onion

4 ounces tomatillos,* husked, rinsed, quartered

1 jalapeño chili, seeded, coarsely chopped

1 garlic clove, chopped

¹/₄ cup chopped fresh cilantro

1 tablespoon fresh lime juice

¹/₄ cup sour cream

12 6-inch-diameter corn tortillas
Pork Chili Verde, chilled (see recipe opposite)

2¹/₄ cups shredded asadero cheese* or Monterey Jack

2 plum tomatoes, seeded, chopped

Char Anaheim chilies over gas flame or in broiler until blackened on all sides. Enclose in plastic bag 10 minutes. Peel, seed and chop chilies.

Combine broth, ¹/₂ cup onion, tomatillos, jalapeño and garlic in medium saucepan. Simmer over medium heat until liquid is reduced to 1 cup, about 10 minutes. Transfer to blender. Cool to room temperature. Add Anaheim chilies, chopped cilantro and lime juice. Blend until smooth.

Transfer to bowl. Whisk in sour cream. Season to taste with salt and pepper. *(Can be made 1 day ahead. Cover; chill.)*

Lightly oil 15x10x2-inch baking dish. Place 6 tortillas between 2 damp paper towels. Cook in microwave on high until warm, about 1 minute. Working with 1 warm tortilla at a time, dip tortillas into sauce; shake excess sauce back into bowl. Place tortillas on work surface. Spoon scant $1/1$ cup Pork Chili Verde, 2 tablespoons cheese and 1 tablespoon onion down center of each. Roll up tortillas. Arrange enchiladas, seam side down, in dish. Repeat with remaining 6 tortillas. *(Can be made 8 hours ahead. Cover enchiladas, remaining sauce and cheese separately. Chill.)* Top enchiladas with remaining sauce, then cheese.

Preheat oven to 350°F. Bake enchiladas uncovered until heated through, 20 minutes (30 minutes if refrigerated). Sprinkle tomatoes over.

*Available at Latin American markets and some supermarkets.

6 SERVINGS

Pork Chili Verde

8   fresh Anaheim chilies*

1   teaspoon cumin seeds

2   tablespoons vegetable oil

1   cup chopped onion

2   pounds trimmed boneless pork shoulder, cut into $1/2$-inch pieces

3   garlic cloves, finely chopped

4   cups water

(handwritten: Make in crock pot)

Char Anaheim chilies over gas flame or in broiler until blackened on all sides. Enclose in plastic bag 10 minutes. Peel, seed and chop chilies.

Stir cumin seeds in heavy small skillet over medium-low heat until fragrant, about 4 minutes. Transfer to spice grinder; process until finely ground.

Heat oil in heavy large pot over medium-high heat. Add onion; sauté 3 minutes. Add pork; cook until juices evaporate and meat browns, stirring often, about 20 minutes. Add chilies, cumin and garlic. Sauté 5 minutes. Add 4 cups water. Simmer uncovered over medium-low heat until meat is very tender and sauce just coats meat, about 1 hour. If necessary, increase heat and continue to simmer until sauce is reduced and just coats meat. Season to taste with salt and pepper. *(Can be prepared 1 day ahead. Cover and chill.)*

*Available at Latin American markets.

MAKES ABOUT 4 CUPS

Tex-Mex Fiesta for Six

Tortilla Soup
(page 32)

Pork Chili Verde Enchiladas
(opposite; pictured opposite)

Black Beans

Mexican Rice

Beer, Margaritas or Sangria

Brownies with Coffee Ice Cream

Red wine, brandy and herbs are reduced to a flavorful sauce in this French classic. This makes a great dinner party dish because the recipe serves ten and it can be prepared a day ahead of time.

3/4 cup all purpose flour

3 4- to 4 1/2-pound chickens, each cut into 8 pieces

4 tablespoons (1/2 stick) butter

4 tablespoons olive oil

5 cups pearl onions, blanched 2 minutes in boiling water, peeled (about 20 ounces)

8 fresh thyme sprigs

4 fresh parsley sprigs

2 bay leaves

2 pounds whole button mushrooms

1 pound carrots (about 6 medium), peeled, cut into 1/3-inch-thick slices

6 garlic cloves, minced

1/2 cup brandy

3 750-ml bottles dry red wine

Place flour in medium bowl. Working in batches, coat chicken with flour; shake off excess. Melt 2 tablespoons butter with 2 tablespoons oil in each of 2 heavy large pots over medium-high heat. Add chicken to pots in batches and cook until brown, turning occasionally, about 8 minutes per batch. Transfer chicken to large bowl.

Add half of onions, thyme, parsley and bay leaves to each pot. Sauté until onions are golden, about 5 minutes. Add half of mushrooms, carrots, garlic and brandy to each pot. Cook until liquid evaporates, scraping up browned bits from bottom of pots. Return chicken to pots. Add 1 1/2 bottles of wine to each pot. Bring to boil. Reduce heat to medium-low. Cover; simmer until chicken is cooked, about 40 minutes. *(Can be made 1 day ahead. Cool slightly. Chill uncovered until cold, then cover and keep chilled. Rewarm over medium heat before continuing.)*

Using tongs, transfer chicken to large shallow serving bowl; tent with foil. Boil cooking liquid in pots until thick enough to coat spoon, about 15 minutes. Spoon sauce and vegetables over chicken and serve.

10 SERVINGS

poultry

Spicy Oven-fried Chicken

1¼ cups buttermilk
¼ cup extra-virgin olive oil
3 tablespoons hot pepper sauce
2 tablespoons Dijon mustard
2 garlic cloves, minced
2 teaspoons salt
½ teaspoon ground black pepper
1 large onion, sliced
12 chicken pieces (breasts, thighs and drumsticks) with skin and bones

1 cup dry unseasoned breadcrumbs
⅓ cup freshly grated Parmesan cheese
¼ cup all purpose flour
2 teaspoons dried thyme
½ teaspoon paprika
½ teaspoon cayenne pepper

3 tablespoons butter, melted

Whisk buttermilk, oil, hot pepper sauce, mustard, garlic, 1 teaspoon salt and ½ teaspoon pepper in large bowl to blend well. Add onion, then chicken and turn to coat. Cover; chill at least 3 hours and up to 1 day, turning chicken occasionally.

Place racks on 2 large rimmed baking sheets. Whisk breadcrumbs, Parmesan cheese, flour, thyme, paprika, cayenne and remaining 1 teaspoon salt in large baking dish to blend. Remove chicken from marinade, allowing excess to drip off. Add chicken to breadcrumb mixture and turn to coat completely. Arrange chicken, skin side up, on racks on baking sheets. Let stand 30 minutes.

Preheat oven to 425°F. Drizzle butter over chicken. Bake until crisp, golden and cooked through, about 50 minutes. Serve warm.

6 SERVINGS

Chicken Marinated in Garlic, Chilies and Citrus Juices

$^1/_2$ cup olive oil
$^1/_3$ cup orange juice
$^1/_4$ cup fresh lime juice
$^1/_4$ cup ground pasilla chilies*
  2   tablespoons ground ancho chilies*
  1   tablespoon minced canned chipotle chilies**
  6   garlic cloves, crushed
  1   onion, chopped
  3   $2^3/_4$- to 3-pound chickens, halved, backbone removed

Whisk oil, orange and lime juices, ground and canned chilies and garlic in 15x10x2-inch baking dish to blend. Mix in onion. Add chicken and turn to coat. Cover and chill at least 4 hours or overnight, turning occasionally.

Prepare barbecue (medium heat). Remove chicken halves from marinade. Sprinkle with salt and pepper. Grill chicken until cooked through, turning occasionally, about 40 minutes.

Ground pasilla and ancho chilies are found in the spice section of some supermarkets. If unavailable, use dried pasilla and ancho chilies, sold in Latin American markets, specialty foods stores and some supermarkets. Seed and stem chilies and finely grind in spice grinder or blender.
**Chipotle chilies canned in a spicy tomato sauce, sometimes called adobo, are available at Latin American markets, specialty foods stores and some supermarkets.*

6 SERVINGS

Chicken and Vegetable Pot Pies with Dilled Biscuit Topping

1   4¹/₂- to 5-pound chicken, quartered, giblets reserved
6   cups canned low-salt chicken broth
1   bay leaf

5   tablespoons butter
³/₄   cup finely chopped red bell pepper
¹/₂   cup chopped onion
³/₄   teaspoon dried thyme
8   ounces button mushrooms, coarsely chopped
5   tablespoons unbleached all purpose flour
1³/₄   cups frozen mixed vegetables (from one 16-ounce bag), thawed
¹/₃   cup whipping cream

Dough for Dilled Buttermilk Biscuits (unbaked; see recipe opposite)

Combine chicken, giblets, broth and bay leaf in large pot. Cover partially; simmer until chicken is just cooked through, rearranging chicken occasionally, about 25 minutes. Transfer chicken to large bowl.

Simmer broth over medium-high heat until reduced to 2¹/₂ cups liquid, about 15 minutes. Strain broth; discard solids. Remove skin and bones from chicken. Tear meat into bite-size pieces; transfer to bowl.

Melt butter in heavy medium saucepan over medium heat. Add bell pepper, onion and thyme. Sauté until onion is tender, about 5 minutes. Add mushrooms. Cook until mushrooms are tender, about 7 minutes. Reduce heat to medium-low. Sprinkle bell pepper mixture with flour; sauté 2 minutes. Gradually whisk in reduced broth. Add mixed vegetables. Simmer until broth thickens, stirring occasionally, about 5 minutes. Remove from heat. Stir chicken and cream into sauce; season with salt and pepper. *(Can be made 1 day ahead. Cool slightly. Cover and chill. Rewarm before continuing.)*

Position rack in top third of oven; preheat to 450°F. Divide chicken mixture among six 1³/₄-cup individual casserole dishes or soufflé dishes. Place 1 unbaked 3-inch square of biscuit dough over each. Bake until filling is bubbling and biscuits are puffed and brown, about 12 minutes. Let stand 5 minutes before serving.

6 SERVINGS

Dilled Buttermilk Biscuits

²/₃ cup chilled buttermilk

1 large egg

3 tablespoons minced fresh dill

2$^{1}/_{2}$ cups unbleached all purpose flour

4 teaspoons baking powder

2 teaspoons sugar

$^{1}/_{4}$ teaspoon salt

$^{1}/_{2}$ cup solid vegetable shortening, chilled, cut into small pieces

7 tablespoons unsalted butter, chilled, cut into small pieces

Preheat oven to 400°F. Whisk buttermilk, egg and dill in small bowl to blend. Whisk flour, baking powder, sugar and salt in large bowl to blend. Add vegetable shortening and butter to dry ingredients; cut in with fork until mixture resembles coarse meal. Add buttermilk mixture and stir just until moist dough forms.

Using floured hands, gently knead dough on well-floured work surface until dough just holds together. Pat out dough to 9x6-inch rectangle (about ³/₄ inch thick). Cut dough into six 3-inch squares. Transfer squares to ungreased baking sheet, spacing 2¹/₂ inches apart. *(Dough can be prepared 8 hours ahead. Cover with plastic wrap and refrigerate.)*

Bake biscuits until puffed and golden brown, about 12 minutes.

MAKES 6

Here, the chicken pot pie filling is divided among small casserole dishes and topped with biscuit dough, then baked. The biscuits are also delicious on their own.

Chicken Normande with Mashed Apples and Potatoes

Country French Menu
for Four

Endive Salad with Toasted
    Walnuts

Chicken Normande with
    Mashed Apples and Potatoes
    (at left; pictured opposite)

Crusty French Bread

White Wine

Hot Lemon Soufflés
    (page 180)

3	cups canned low-salt chicken broth
1	cup apple cider or apple juice
8	ounces parsnips, peeled, cut into $1/2$-inch cubes
$1^3/_4$	pounds Yukon Gold potatoes, peeled, cut into $1/2$-inch cubes
$3/_4$	pound Golden Delicious apples (about 2 large), peeled, cored, cut into $1/2$-inch cubes
5	tablespoons butter
8	skinless boneless chicken thighs, cut into 1-inch pieces
6	teaspoons minced fresh thyme
2	tablespoons all purpose flour
1	cup frozen peas, thawed
$1/_3$	cup brandy
$1/_3$	cup whipping cream

Combine first 3 ingredients in large pot and bring to boil. Reduce heat to medium, cover and simmer until parsnips are tender, about 5 minutes. Using slotted spoon, transfer parsnips to small bowl. Add potatoes and apples to same pot. Cover; simmer until very tender, about 20 minutes. Remove from heat. Using slotted spoon, transfer potatoes and apples to large bowl; add 3 tablespoons butter. Mash until almost smooth. Season with salt and pepper. Pour broth mixture into medium bowl; reserve pot.

Sprinkle chicken with salt, pepper and 4 teaspoons thyme; dust with flour. Melt remaining 2 tablespoons butter in reserved pot over medium-high heat. Add half of chicken. Sauté until brown and cooked through, turning with tongs, about 5 minutes. Using slotted spoon, transfer sautéed chicken to 11x7x2-inch glass baking dish. Repeat with remaining chicken. Top with parsnips, remaining 2 teaspoons thyme and peas.

Return broth mixture to same pot; add brandy and whipping cream. Boil over medium-high heat until sauce is reduced to $1^1/4$ cups, scraping up browned bits, about 3 minutes. Season with salt and pepper. Spoon over chicken. Cover with potato-apple mixture. *(Can be prepared 1 day ahead. Refrigerate until cold, then cover and keep refrigerated.)*

Preheat oven to 350°F. Bake casserole uncovered until potato topping is crusty and chicken filling is heated through, about 35 minutes (about 45 minutes if refrigerated). Serve warm.

4 TO 6 SERVINGS

Grilled Chicken with Oregano, Cinnamon and Paprika

Here, spiced grilled chicken is topped with a fresh tomato compote. For the best flavor, begin this recipe the day before you plan to serve it.

 3 tablespoons fresh lemon juice
 3 tablespoons extra-virgin olive oil
 2 tablespoons chopped fresh oregano
 $^3/_4$ teaspoon salt
 $^3/_4$ teaspoon ground black pepper
 $^1/_2$ teaspoon ground cinnamon
 $^1/_2$ teaspoon paprika
 6 skinless boneless chicken breast halves

 Nonstick vegetable oil spray
 Tomato and Red Onion Compote (see recipe below)

Whisk first 7 ingredients to blend in 13x9x2-inch glass baking dish. Add chicken to dish and turn to coat. Let stand at room temperature 1 hour, turning occasionally. *(Can be made 1 day ahead. Cover and refrigerate.)*

Spray grill rack with nonstick spray; prepare barbecue (medium-high heat). Grill chicken until cooked through, turning occasionally, about 15 minutes. Transfer to plates. Serve with compote.

6 SERVINGS

Tomato and Red Onion Compote

 2 tablespoons extra-virgin olive oil
 $1^1/_2$ cups chopped tomatoes
 $^1/_3$ cup chopped red onion
 3 tablespoons chopped fresh oregano

Heat oil in heavy large skillet over medium-high heat. Add tomatoes, red onion and oregano and sauté just until heated through, about 2 minutes. Season to taste with salt and pepper.

MAKES ABOUT $1^1/_2$ CUPS

Roasted Chicken, Zucchini and Ricotta Sandwiches on Focaccia

- 2 medium zucchini, shredded
- 2 teaspoons salt

- 1 tablespoon olive oil
- 1 15-ounce container whole-milk ricotta cheese
- $^1/_4$ cup freshly grated Parmesan cheese
- 1 teaspoon grated lemon peel

- 4 5x4-inch pieces focaccia or ciabatta, halved horizontally

- 2 large tomatoes, thinly sliced
- 4 purchased roasted chicken breasts, skinned, boned, thinly sliced crosswise

Mix zucchini and salt in medium bowl. Transfer to colander; set over bowl. Let stand 15 minutes to drain liquid from zucchini. Rinse and drain zucchini. Squeeze zucchini to remove liquid.

Heat oil in large skillet over medium heat. Add zucchini and sauté 2 minutes. Cool slightly. Add ricotta, Parmesan and lemon peel to zucchini. Stir to blend. Season mixture to taste with salt and pepper. *(Can be made 8 hours ahead. Cover and refrigerate.)*

Preheat broiler. Arrange focaccia pieces cut side up on baking sheet. Broil focaccia just until lightly toasted. Spread ricotta mixture generously over all toasted focaccia pieces. Broil until ricotta mixture is heated through and beginning to brown in spots, about 4 minutes.

Top 4 focaccia pieces with tomato, then chicken, dividing equally. Sprinkle with salt and pepper. Cover with remaining focaccia, ricotta-mixture-side down. Cut sandwiches diagonally in half and serve.

4 SERVINGS

Chicken Breasts with
Sun-dried Tomato and Garlic Crust

2 cups fresh breadcrumbs made from French bread

$1/2$ cup drained oil-packed sun-dried tomatoes, $3^{1}/_{2}$ tablespoons oil reserved

2 large garlic cloves

4 12-ounce chicken breast halves with skin and bone

Combine breadcrumbs, sun-dried tomatoes, 2 tablespoons oil reserved from tomatoes and garlic in processor. Using on/off turns, process until tomatoes are coarsely chopped. Season to taste with salt and pepper. *(Can be made 8 hours ahead. Cover and chill.)*

Preheat oven to 375°F. Sprinkle chicken with salt and pepper. Heat $1^{1}/_{2}$ tablespoons oil reserved from tomatoes in heavy large skillet over medium-high heat. Add chicken, skin side down, and cook until skin is crisp and golden, about 5 minutes.

Transfer chicken, skin side up, to heavy rimmed baking sheet. Spoon breadcrumb mixture atop chicken, dividing equally and pressing to adhere. Bake until chicken is cooked through, about 30 minutes.

Transfer chicken to plates and serve.

4 SERVINGS

Chicken with Prosciutto and Sage

2 chicken breast halves with skin and bones
2 tablespoons olive oil
$^1/_2$ cup finely chopped onion
$^1/_4$ cup finely chopped carrot
$^1/_4$ cup finely chopped celery
$^1/_2$ cup dry white wine
$^1/_4$ cup (packed) slivered prosciutto (about 1$^1/_2$ ounces)
1$^1/_2$ tablespoons chopped fresh sage or 1$^1/_2$ teaspoons dried

Sprinkle chicken with salt and pepper. Heat oil in heavy medium skillet over medium-high heat. Add chicken and sauté until brown, about 3 minutes per side. Transfer chicken to plate. Add onion, carrot and celery to skillet; sauté until vegetables begin to brown, about 5 minutes. Return chicken and any accumulated juices to skillet; add wine, prosciutto and sage. Bring to boil. Reduce heat to medium-low. Cover; simmer until chicken is cooked through, about 6 minutes per side. Serve with sauce.

2 SERVINGS

This easy entrée requires less than 15 minutes of cooking time. The chicken and vegetables are browned separately, then all of the ingredients are simmered together briefly. Try the recipe with duck breasts for something different.

Smoked Turkey Sandwiches with Orange-Cranberry Sauce

1 medium sweet onion (such as Maui), thinly sliced
3 tablespoons apple cider vinegar
2 tablespoons chopped fresh dill
2 teaspoons sugar
$^3/_4$ cup canned whole-berry cranberry sauce
1$^1/_2$ teaspoons grated orange peel

8 slices whole grain bread, toasted
8 ounces thinly sliced smoked turkey breast
1 bunch watercress, thick stems trimmed

Mix onion, vinegar, dill and sugar in medium bowl. Season with salt and pepper. Mix cranberry sauce and orange peel in small bowl.

Place toast slices on work surface. Spread cranberry mixture over slices, dividing equally. Top 4 slices with onion mixture, then turkey and watercress, dividing equally. Top with 4 toast slices, cranberry side down.

4 SERVINGS

The flavors in these sandwiches are reminiscent of Thanksgiving dinner. Make them with leftover roast turkey, if you have any on hand.

Cornish Game Hens with Pancetta, Juniper Berries and Beets

4 medium beets with greens, beets peeled and cut into $1/2$-inch pieces, greens finely chopped
$1/2$ pound $1/4$-inch-thick pancetta,* finely chopped
1 tablespoon juniper berries, coarsely chopped
4 $1^1/_2$- to $1^3/_4$-pound Cornish game hens, giblets removed
3 tablespoons olive oil

Position 1 rack in top third of oven and second rack in bottom third of oven and preheat to 375°F. Mix $1^1/_2$ cups chopped beet greens, pancetta and juniper berries in medium bowl. Season to taste with salt and pepper. Fill hen cavities with pancetta mixture, dividing equally. Tie hen legs together. Place hens in heavy large roasting pan. Rub 1 tablespoon olive oil over hens. Sprinkle hens with salt and pepper. *(Can be prepared 8 hours ahead. Cover and refrigerate.)*

Roast hens on bottom rack in oven until golden and juices run clear when thickest part of thigh is pierced, about 1 hour 15 minutes.

Meanwhile, toss beets with remaining 2 tablespoons olive oil on heavy large baking sheet. Season with salt and pepper. Arrange beets in single layer. Roast beets on top rack in oven until tender and beginning to caramelize, stirring occasionally, about 45 minutes.

Transfer hens to plates. Remove string. Scrape up any browned bits from bottom of roasting pan. Pour pan juices through sieve into 2-cup glass measuring cup. Spoon fat off top of pan juices.

Spoon beets around hens. Drizzle pan juices around hens and serve.

Pancetta, Italian bacon cured in salt, is available at Italian markets and some specialty foods stores nationwide.

4 SERVINGS

Elegant Dinner for Four

Penne Tossed with Butter and Grated Fontina Cheese

Cornish Game Hens with Pancetta, Juniper Berries and Beets
(at left; pictured opposite)

Lentils with Port-glazed Shallots
(page 128; pictured opposite)

Sautéed Beet Greens

Moulin-à-Vent

Cherries Simmered in Red Wine
(page 164)

Duck with Pine Nuts and Olives

Fresh duck is generally available only from late spring through early winter, but frozen ducks work well in this recipe, too. Ducks are fattier than chicken and turkey, so it's necessary to remove the excess fat during roasting, and to degrease the pan juices before using them in a sauce, as detailed in this recipe.

SAUCE

- 1 tablespoon butter
- 2 ducks (each about 5^1/$_4$ pounds), fresh or frozen, thawed (necks, hearts and gizzards reserved)
- 2 carrots, chopped
- 1 onion, chopped
- 1 fresh thyme sprig
- 1 bay leaf
- 1 cup dry white wine
- 6 cups water

DUCK

- ^{1}/$_4$ cup fresh lemon juice
- ^{1}/$_2$ cup (1 stick) chilled butter, cut into small pieces
- 12 green olives, pitted, halved
- 12 Kalamata olives or other brine-cured black olives, pitted, halved
- ^{1}/$_4$ cup pine nuts, toasted

FOR SAUCE: Melt butter in heavy large saucepan over medium heat. Add duck necks, hearts and gizzards; sauté until brown, 15 minutes. Add carrots, onion, thyme and bay leaf. Sauté until onion is translucent, 8 minutes. Add wine; simmer until reduced by half, 5 minutes. Add 6 cups water. Simmer uncovered until mixture is reduced to 5^1/$_2$ cups, 1 hour. Strain into medium saucepan. Simmer gently over medium-low heat until reduced to 1^1/$_2$ cups, 1 hour. *(Can be made 1 day ahead. Cover; chill.)*

FOR DUCK: Preheat oven to 400°F. Trim excess fat from cavity of each duck. Using fork, pierce duck skin in several places. Place ducks, breast side up, on rack in large roasting pan. Sprinkle with salt and pepper. Roast 40 minutes, basting frequently with pan juices and removing excess fat. Turn ducks breast side down on rack and roast 25 minutes. Turn ducks breast side up again and roast until deep golden brown and thermometer inserted into thickest part of thigh registers 170°F, about 15 minutes longer.

Transfer ducks to platter. Tent with foil. Pour juices from roasting pan into 4-cup glass measuring cup, scraping up any browned bits. Freeze juices 15 minutes. Spoon fat off top; discard. Add pan juices and lemon juice to sauce. Simmer until reduced to 1^1/$_4$ cups, 5 minutes. Remove from heat.

Preheat broiler. Cut leg-thigh pieces off each duck. Remove breast meat. Place leg-thigh and breast pieces on baking sheet. Broil until skin is crisp and dark golden, about 2 minutes. Cut breasts into thin slices. Arrange 1 leg-thigh piece and 1 sliced duck breast on each plate.

Bring sauce to simmer over low heat. Add butter; whisk just until melted. Mix in all olives and pine nuts. Season to taste with salt and pepper. Spoon sauce over duck and serve.

4 SERVINGS

Duck Breasts with Orange, Honey and Tea Sauce

2 boneless Muscovy duck breast halves (about 1$^3/_4$ pounds total)

$^3/_4$ cup chopped shallots

2$^1/_4$ cups canned low-salt chicken broth

1$^1/_2$ cups orange juice

4$^1/_2$ teaspoons Earl Grey tea leaves or 5 tea bags, leaves removed from bags

1 tablespoon honey

3 tablespoons butter, cut into small pieces

Orange segments (optional)

Preheat oven to 450°F. Pierce skin of duck breasts all over with fork. Sprinkle duck with salt and pepper. Heat heavy large skillet over high heat. Add duck breasts, skin side down, to skillet. Cook until skin is well browned, about 4 minutes. Turn duck breasts over; cook 2 minutes. Remove from heat. Set rack in roasting pan. Transfer duck breasts to rack (reserve drippings in skillet). Roast duck breasts to desired doneness, about 20 minutes for medium-rare.

Meanwhile, heat drippings in skillet over medium heat. Add shallots and sauté until beginning to brown, about 5 minutes. Tilt skillet; push shallots to higher end of skillet, allowing drippings to flow to lower end. Spoon off drippings and discard. Add broth, orange juice and tea leaves to skillet. Boil until mixture is reduced to 1$^1/_4$ cups, about 17 minutes. Pour mixture through strainer set over bowl, pressing on solids to extract as much liquid as possible. Discard solids in strainer. Return liquid to same skillet. Add honey; bring to simmer. Whisk in butter. Season sauce to taste with salt and pepper. Thinly slice duck breasts crosswise. Fan slices on each of 4 plates, dividing equally. Spoon sauce around duck. Garnish with orange segments, if desired, and serve immediately.

4 SERVINGS

Cooking with Tea

Although people around the world drink gallons of tea, the beverage and the fragrant leaves from which it derives do not play a great role in any one country's cuisine, with the possible exception of China. That country brought us such delicacies as tea-smoked duck and green tea ice cream. Certainly the potential uses of tea in Western cookery have not been well explored.

Tea can contribute to other foods the same qualities that are most often appreciated when it is sipped from a cup. Try using bergamot-scented Earl Grey tea leaves to flavor the sauce for duck, straining out the leaves after they have steeped in the liquid, as in Duck Breasts with Orange, Honey and Tea Sauce (at left). Or use flavorful brewed black tea as the soaking liquid for the dried fruit that embellishes baked goods. Flowery-tasting jasmine tea makes a lovely poaching liquid for fresh fruit. And any strongly brewed tea may be combined with sparkling water, citrus juice or frozen lemonade concentrate and, if you wish, a favorite liquor, to make a delightfully refreshing punch.

seafood

Baked Salmon with Cucumber-Watercress Relish

CUCUMBER-WATERCRESS RELISH

    2   teaspoons yellow mustard seeds
  $^3/_4$ teaspoon fennel seeds
  $^1/_4$ cup white wine vinegar
    2   tablespoons olive oil
    1   tablespoon sugar
  $2^1/_4$ cups $^1/_4$-inch pieces unpeeled seeded English hothouse cucumber
    1   cup chopped red onion
  $^1/_2$ cup coarsely chopped watercress

SALMON

    6   tablespoons ($^3/_4$ stick) butter
    2   tablespoons chopped fresh tarragon
    4   teaspoons fennel seeds, crushed
    1   tablespoon grated lemon peel
    1   tablespoon fresh lemon juice
    6   6- to 7-ounce salmon fillets

    6   very thin lemon slices
    6   fresh tarragon sprigs

FOR CUCUMBER-WATERCRESS RELISH: Stir mustard seeds and fennel seeds in small skillet over medium-high heat until mustard seeds begin to pop, about 2 minutes. Transfer to medium glass bowl. Whisk in vinegar, oil and sugar. Add cucumber and onion; toss to combine. Season with salt and pepper. Let stand at room temperature 30 minutes, stirring occasionally. *(Can be made 4 hours ahead. Cover and refrigerate.)* Mix chopped watercress into relish.

FOR SALMON: Stir butter, chopped tarragon, fennel seeds, lemon peel and lemon juice in small saucepan over low heat until butter melts. Season with salt and pepper. Arrange salmon on baking sheet. Brush butter mixture over salmon. *(Can be made 8 hours ahead. Cover; chill.)*

Position rack in center of oven and preheat to 450°F. Bake salmon fillets until just opaque in center, about 12 minutes. Transfer salmon to plates. Garnish with lemon slices and fresh tarragon sprigs. Serve immediately with cucumber-watercress relish.

6 SERVINGS

Cal-Asian Seared Tuna Sandwiches

$^1/_2$ cup mayonnaise
  3 tablespoons finely chopped green onions
  2 teaspoons minced peeled fresh ginger
  1 teaspoon soy sauce
  1 teaspoon oriental sesame oil

  4 $^3/_4$-inch-thick tuna steaks (each about 5 ounces)
  1 tablespoon vegetable oil

  8 $^1/_2$-inch-thick slices crusty country-style white bread
$^1/_2$ medium English hothouse cucumber, unpeeled, thinly sliced
  8 radishes, thinly sliced
  1 ripe avocado, pitted, peeled, sliced

Mix first 5 ingredients in small bowl to blend. *(Can be prepared 1 day ahead. Cover and refrigerate.)*

Sprinkle tuna with salt and pepper. Heat vegetable oil in heavy large skillet over medium-high heat. Add tuna and cook to desired doneness, about 2 minutes per side for medium-rare.

Spread mayonnaise mixture over 1 side of each bread slice. Top 4 bread slices with cucumber, radishes, then avocado, dividing equally. Sprinkle with salt and pepper. Top with tuna. Place remaining bread slices, mayonnaise side down, atop tuna. Cut sandwiches in half and serve.

4 SERVINGS

Sautéed Cod with Asparagus Sauce and Fennel

$2^1/_2$ pounds asparagus, trimmed
  6 tablespoons ($^3/_4$ stick) unsalted butter

  6 6- to 7-ounce cod fillets

  2 teaspoons fennel seeds, coarsely chopped

Cut asparagus tips into $2^3/_4$-inch-long pieces; set aside. Peel asparagus stalks. Cut stalks into 1-inch pieces. Cook stalks in large saucepan of boiling slightly salted water until very tender, about 10 minutes. Using slotted spoon, transfer stalks to blender. Add $^3/_4$ cup cooking liquid to blender. Blend until very smooth, adding more cooking liquid to thin sauce. Blend 2 tablespoons butter into sauce. Season with salt and pepper. *(Sauce can be made 8 hours ahead. Cover and refrigerate.)*

Transfer sauce to medium saucepan. Bring sauce to simmer. Remove from heat. Cover to keep warm. Cook asparagus tips in boiling salted water until crisp-tender, about 4 minutes. Drain.

Sprinkle fish with salt and pepper. Melt 2 tablespoons butter in each of 2 heavy large skillets over medium-high heat. Add 3 fish fillets to each skillet and cook until golden and opaque in center, about 4 minutes per side.

Spoon warm sauce onto plates. Top with fish. Garnish with asparagus tips. Sprinkle with fennel seeds and serve.

6 SERVINGS

Chinese-Style Steamed Fish

2 6-ounce red snapper fillets
2 tablespoons dry white wine
$1^1/_2$ teaspoons minced peeled fresh ginger
2 small garlic cloves, minced
4 teaspoons soy sauce
$1^1/_2$ teaspoons oriental sesame oil
2 tablespoons chopped fresh cilantro

Place small cake rack in large (12-inch-diameter) skillet; place 9-inch-diameter glass pie dish on rack. Put fish in dish; sprinkle lightly with salt and pepper. Sprinkle wine, ginger and garlic in dish around fish. Top fish with soy sauce, sesame oil and 1 tablespoon cilantro. Pour enough water into skillet to reach depth of 1 inch. Bring water to boil. Cover skillet; steam fish until just opaque in center, about 10 minutes. Transfer fish to plates; top with juices from dish and remaining 1 tablespoon cilantro.

2 SERVINGS

The classic Chinese way to steam fish is in a bamboo steamer set over boiling water in a wok. Here, that method is adapted to more familiar equipment—a pie dish is set atop a cake rack inside a skillet. Water is added to the skillet and brought to a boil, then the skillet is covered so that the steam cooks the fish.

Roasted Sea Bass with
Tomato Coulis and Fennel Salsa

TOMATO COULIS

2¹/₂ pounds ripe tomatoes, halved, seeded, chopped

4¹/₂ tablespoons extra-virgin olive oil

3 tablespoons balsamic vinegar

FISH

¹/₄ cup extra-virgin olive oil

2 teaspoons balsamic vinegar

10 5- to 6-ounce sea bass fillets

All purpose flour

Fennel Salsa (see recipe below)

Fresh basil sprigs

FOR TOMATO COULIS: Blend tomatoes in processor until almost smooth. Gradually blend in oil, then vinegar. Process until smooth, scraping down sides of bowl. Season with salt and pepper. Transfer to bowl. *(Can be made 1 day ahead. Cover and refrigerate. Whisk before using.)*

FOR FISH: Whisk oil and vinegar to blend in 13x9x2-inch glass baking dish. Sprinkle fish with salt and pepper. Place fish in marinade in dish; turn to coat. Chill at least 1 hour and up to 2 hours.

Position 1 rack in top third and 1 rack in bottom third of oven and preheat to 400°F. Place 1 large rimmed baking sheet on each rack and heat 15 minutes. Dust flat side of each fillet with flour. Brush each heated baking sheet generously with oil. Place 5 fillets, floured side down, on each prepared sheet. Roast until just opaque in center, about 12 minutes.

Spoon 3 tablespoons coulis onto center of each plate. Top with fish. Spoon Fennel Salsa alongside. Garnish with basil and serve.

10 SERVINGS

Fennel Salsa

3 cups finely diced fresh fennel bulbs (about 2 small)

1 cup diced seeded tomatoes

²/₃ cup chopped pitted Kalamata olives or other brine-cured black olives

¹/₄ cup chopped fresh basil

3 tablespoons extra-virgin olive oil

2 tablespoons drained capers, chopped

1 tablespoon balsamic vinegar

Combine all ingredients in large bowl and toss to blend. Season salsa to taste with salt and pepper. Cover salsa with plastic wrap and refrigerate at least 2 hours and up to 1 day, tossing occasionally.

MAKES ABOUT 4 CUPS

Fisherman's Soup

    3   tablespoons olive oil
    1   medium onion, finely chopped
 $1/2$ cup chopped celery
    2   garlic cloves, finely chopped
    1   pound plum tomatoes, peeled, chopped
 $1/4$ cup chopped fresh parsley
    2   tablespoons chopped fresh rosemary
 $1/2$ teaspoon dried crushed red pepper
    1   tablespoon all purpose flour
 $3/4$ cup dry white wine
    6   cups water

    1   8-ounce orange roughy fillet, cut into 2-inch pieces
    1   8-ounce sea bass fillet, cut into 2-inch pieces
    8   ounces uncooked large shrimp, peeled, deveined
    4   ounces cleaned squid, bodies cut into $1/2$-inch-wide rings, tentacles left whole

        Additional chopped fresh parsley
        Sea salt
        Extra-virgin olive oil

This seafood soup is a specialty of Livorno, a port city in Tuscany. To serve it as they do there, place a slice of toasted bread in each bowl before ladling the soup.

Heat 3 tablespoons oil in large pot over medium heat. Add onion, celery and garlic. Sauté 10 minutes. Stir in next 4 ingredients. Sauté 2 minutes. Sprinkle flour over. Stir 2 minutes. Add wine; cook until liquid evaporates. Add 6 cups water. Bring to boil. Reduce heat; simmer 20 minutes.

Add all seafood to soup base. Cook just until opaque in center, about 3 minutes. Season to taste with salt.

Ladle soup into 4 bowls. Sprinkle with additional parsley and sea salt. Drizzle soup with olive oil and serve.

4 SERVINGS

Salmon Club Sandwich

6 tablespoons mayonnaise
5 tablespoons minced fresh basil
1 teaspoon grated lemon peel

3 tablespoons olive oil
1 tablespoon fresh lemon juice
4 5- to 6-ounce skinless salmon fillets (each about $^3/_4$ inch thick)

8 bacon slices
1 small red onion, sliced

8 $^1/_2$-inch-thick sourdough or country-style white bread slices
  (each about 5x3 inches)
8 tomato slices
8 lettuce leaves

Mix mayonnaise, 2 tablespoons basil and lemon peel in small bowl to blend. *(Can be made 1 day ahead. Cover and chill.)*

Mix remaining 3 tablespoons basil, olive oil and lemon juice in large glass baking dish. Add salmon to oil mixture; turn to coat. Cover with plastic wrap and refrigerate 1 to 4 hours.

Cook bacon slices in heavy large skillet over medium-high heat until crisp. Using tongs, transfer bacon to paper towels to drain. Add sliced onion to bacon drippings in skillet. Sauté until onion is tender and beginning to brown, about 5 minutes.

Prepare barbecue (medium-high heat). Grill marinated salmon until just opaque in center, about 3 minutes per side. Grill bread slices just until golden, about 2 minutes per side.

Spread mayonnaise mixture over 1 side of bread slices. Top each of 4 bread slices with 2 bacon slices, 2 tomato slices, 1/4 of onion, 1 salmon fillet and 2 lettuce leaves. Cover with remaining bread slices and serve.

4 SERVINGS

Crab Salad with
Buttermilk Caesar Dressing

7 garlic cloves
5 anchovy fillets, drained, chopped
3/4 cup mayonnaise
1/4 cup buttermilk
1 tablespoon fresh lemon juice
1 teaspoon Worcestershire sauce

1/4 cup olive oil
3 cups 1-inch cubes crustless day-old sourdough bread

1 pound fresh lump crabmeat, picked over
14 cups bite-size pieces romaine lettuce (about 10 ounces)
3 cups mixed baby greens
1/3 cup freshly grated Parmesan cheese

Finely chop 3 garlic cloves and anchovies in processor. Add mayonnaise, buttermilk, lemon juice and Worcestershire and blend until smooth. Season dressing to taste with pepper.

Heat oil in large skillet over medium-low heat. Flatten 4 garlic cloves with flat side of knife blade. Add to oil; cook until brown, about 5 minutes. Using slotted spoon, discard garlic. Add bread to oil; sauté until crisp and golden, about 15 minutes. Transfer to paper towels; drain.

Toss crab and 1/4 cup dressing in medium bowl. Combine romaine, greens, cheese and bread cubes in large bowl. Toss with enough dressing to taste. Season generously with pepper. Divide among plates. Top with crab and serve.

4 SERVINGS

Sautéed Shrimp on Parmesan Grits

6 tablespoons (³/₄ stick) butter
4 ounces ham, diced (about 1 cup)
1¹/₂ cups sliced stemmed shiitake mushrooms
1 cup finely chopped green bell pepper
¹/₂ cup minced onion
2 teaspoons minced fresh thyme
1 cup canned low-salt chicken broth
¹/₂ cup freshly brewed hot coffee
¹/₂ cup seeded chopped tomatoes
1 teaspoon hot pepper sauce
¹/₄ cup Madeira
2 teaspoons cornstarch
1 pound large uncooked shrimp, peeled, deveined
Parmesan Grits (see recipe below)
Freshly grated Parmesan cheese

Melt 2 tablespoons butter in heavy large skillet over medium-high heat. Add ham; sauté until brown, about 2 minutes. Add mushrooms, pepper, onion and thyme; sauté 3 minutes. Add broth and next 3 ingredients; bring to boil. Mix Madeira and cornstarch in small bowl. Add to sauce and bring to boil, stirring constantly. Reduce heat; simmer until thickened, about 3 minutes. Season gravy with salt and pepper.

Melt 3 tablespoons butter in heavy large skillet over medium-high heat. Add shrimp; sauté until opaque in center, about 3 minutes. Add gravy; bring to simmer. Add 1 tablespoon butter; stir until melted. Divide grits among plates. Spoon shrimp and gravy over. Sprinkle with cheese.

4 SERVINGS

Parmesan Grits

3 cups water
1 cup milk
1 cup quick-cooking grits
1 teaspoon salt
¹/₂ cup freshly grated Parmesan cheese

Bring first 4 ingredients to boil in heavy large saucepan, whisking constantly. Reduce heat, cover and simmer until grits are creamy, stirring occasionally, about 10 minutes. Add cheese; whisk until melted.

4 SERVINGS

With the popularity of Italian cooking, many people have come to know and like polenta, also known as corn grits, the cornmeal mush of Northern Italy. This familiarity has paved the way for hominy grits, polenta's American cousin. Hominy grits, once rarely seen outside the South, have started showing up on restaurant menus around the country.

While polenta uses coarse cornmeal ground from dried yellow or sometimes white corn, hominy grits come from dried white hominy—corn that has been treated with slaked lime or lye to soften and remove its hull and germ. Surprisingly, grits are not named for their texture; the word comes from Middle English *gyrt*, meaning "bran."

Mildly earthy and slightly sweet in flavor, hominy grits are cooked in water or milk to a thick, porridge-like consistency, and are served as a breakfast side dish, much as potatoes would be, or as a side for lunch or dinner. For the best flavor, look for coarse stone-ground grits, which require about 40 minutes of simmering. Also available are regular coarsely ground grits, which cook in about 20 minutes, and fine-textured quick-cooking grits, which have been precooked and redried, and need only five to ten minutes to cook.

Shrimp and Mango Skewers with Guava-Lime Glaze

  3 tablespoons olive oil
  1 tablespoon minced peeled fresh ginger
  2 garlic cloves, minced
  1 teaspoon dried crushed red pepper
 18 uncooked colossal shrimp or 36 jumbo shrimp (about 2 pounds), peeled,
     tails left intact, deveined
  2 red bell peppers, each cut into 12 pieces
  2 firm but ripe mangoes, peeled, pitted, each cut into 12 wedges
  6 12-inch bamboo skewers (for colossal shrimp) or twelve 12-inch bamboo
     skewers (for jumbo shrimp), soaked in water 30 minutes, drained

     Guava-Lime Glaze (see recipe below)

Prepare barbecue (medium-high heat). Mix first 4 ingredients in large bowl. Add shrimp, bell peppers and mangoes; toss to coat. Alternate bell pepper, mango and 3 colossal shrimp on each of 6 skewers, or alternate bell pepper, mango and 3 jumbo shrimp on each of 12 skewers. *(Can be prepared 4 hours ahead. Cover and chill.)*

Grill shrimp until cooked through, brushing with Guava-Lime Glaze during last 2 minutes, cooking colossal shrimp about 4 minutes per side or jumbo shrimp about 3 minutes per side.

6 SERVINGS

Guava-Lime Glaze

  2 cups canned guava nectar
  1 cup orange juice
 $^{1}/_{2}$ cup red wine vinegar
 $^{1}/_{3}$ cup fresh lime juice

Combine nectar, orange juice and vinegar in heavy medium saucepan. Boil until reduced to $^{2}/_{3}$ cup, about 30 minutes. Cool completely. Mix in lime juice. *(Can be made 1 day ahead. Cover and chill.)*

MAKES 1 CUP

Asian Barbecue for Six

Grilled Chicken Wings

Shrimp and Mango Skewers with
  Guava-Lime Glaze
  (at left; pictured opposite)

Japanese-Style Quick-pickled Slaw
  (page 146; pictured opposite)

Steamed Rice

Grilled Eggplant and Onions

Beer, Gewürztraminer or
  Chenin Blanc

Flan

Shopping for Shellfish

One key rule applies to shellfish: Whatever you buy should have the fresh, clean scent of the sea, without any "off" odors. Always use a reputable fishmonger, with a rapid turnover of inventory, and keep the following in mind.

- Lobsters: Choose lively lobsters. Female lobsters are said to have sweeter flesh—and they often contain rich, delicious red eggs called coral or roe. Check the small fins, called swimmerets, on the abdomen. Delicate swimmerets indicate a female; thick ones denote a male.
- Crabs: Crab is usually sold already cooked because the raw meat keeps for only 24 hours. Ask for crab that wasn't frozen after cooking; that process diminishes the sweetness and firmness of the meat.
- Shrimp: Most raw shrimp in markets were probably frozen on the ship when they were caught, then defrosted for sale. To eliminate the ammonia-like smell such shrimp sometimes develop, soak them in lightly salted fresh cold water for 15 minutes, then drain, rinse and cook.
- Oysters, Clams and Mussels: Choose specimens with tightly closed shells or shells that close quickly when tapped. Avoid any with cracked shells. Shellfish are at their peak in autumn and winter.

Grilled Lobster with Ginger Butter

2 1^1/$_2$- to 2-pound live lobsters

Olive oil
Chipotle-Lime Oil (see recipe below)
Ginger-Green Onion Butter (see recipe opposite)

Drop 1 lobster, head first, into large pot of boiling water. Cover; cook 3 minutes (lobster will not be fully cooked). Using tongs, transfer lobster to baking sheet. Return water to boil. Repeat with second lobster.

Transfer 1 lobster, shell side down, to work surface. Place tip of large knife into center of lobster. Cut lengthwise in half from center to end of head (knife may not cut through shell), then cut in half from center to end of tail. Use poultry shears to cut shell. Repeat with second lobster.

Prepare barbecue (medium-high heat). Keeping lobster halves meat side up, brush shells with olive oil. Place halves, meat side up, on barbecue. Brush meat with oil; sprinkle with salt and pepper. Place pans with sauces at edge of barbecue to rewarm. Cover barbecue; grill lobsters until just opaque in thickest portion of tail, about 7 to 9 minutes. Serve, passing warm sauces separately.

2 SERVINGS

Chipotle-Lime Oil

^{1}/$_2$ cup olive oil
6 large garlic cloves, chopped
1 tablespoon fresh lime juice
1^1/$_2$ teaspoons minced canned chipotle chilies*
1 teaspoon grated lime peel
^{3}/$_4$ teaspoon salt
2 tablespoons chopped fresh cilantro

Cook oil and garlic in heavy small saucepan over medium-low heat until garlic begins to brown, about 8 minutes. Carefully mix in next 4 ingredients. Stir until salt dissolves. Remove from heat. *(Can be made 2 hours ahead. Let stand at room temperature.)* Mix in cilantro.

*Chipotle *chilies canned in a spicy tomato sauce, sometimes called adobo, are available at Latin American markets, specialty foods stores and some supermarkets.*

MAKES ABOUT ^{2}/$_3$ CUP

The Flavors of Bon Appétit 2001

Ginger-Green Onion Butter

    2   tablespoons peanut oil
    2   teaspoons (packed) minced peeled fresh ginger
  1/4   cup Chinese rice wine or sake
  1/3   cup finely chopped green onions
    3   tablespoons butter, room temperature

Cook oil and ginger in small saucepan over medium-low heat 2 minutes. Carefully add wine; simmer until reduced by half. Remove from heat. Stir in green onions and butter. Season with salt and pepper. *(Can be made 2 hours ahead. Let stand at room temperature.)*

MAKES ABOUT 1/2 CUP

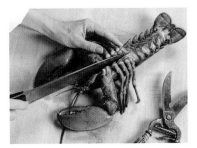

After boiling the lobsters for a few minutes, split them in half lengthwise for grilling. Place one lobster, shell side down and head facing you, on the work surface. Insert the tip of a chef's knife into the center, and cut the lobster down the middle from the center to the end of the head.

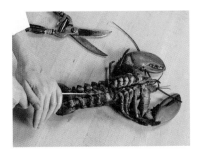

Turn the lobster around so that the tail is facing you, and insert the knife into the center again. This time, cut the lobster down the middle from the center to the end of the tail.

If the chef's knife does not cut all the way through the hard shell, use poultry shears (heavy-duty kitchen scissors).

Shrimp Remoulade with Avocado and Hearts of Palm

Hearty enough for a main course, this recipe would also make a terrific starter for up to 12. Note that artichoke hearts can be used in place of hearts of palm, if desired.

$^3/_4$ cup olive oil
$^1/_2$ cup chopped onion
$^1/_2$ cup Creole mustard
$^1/_4$ cup tarragon vinegar
3 garlic cloves
2 teaspoons paprika
1 teaspoon salt
$^3/_4$ teaspoon cayenne pepper
$^3/_4$ cup coarsely chopped green onions

5 cups shredded romaine lettuce (from 1 large head)
2 pounds cooked peeled deveined large shrimp
1 14.4-ounce jar diced hearts of palm, drained, or one 13- to 14-ounce can artichoke hearts, drained, halved
3 avocados, halved, pitted, peeled, diced

Combine first 8 ingredients in processor and blend well. Add green onions and blend mixture just until onions are finely chopped. *(Sauce can be made 2 days ahead. Cover and refrigerate.)*

Put sauce in bowl and set in center of platter. Surround with lettuce. Top lettuce with shrimp, hearts of palm and avocados and serve.

6 SERVINGS

Curried Scallop and Vegetable Chowder

2	tablespoons ($^1/_4$ stick) butter
$1^1/_2$	cups chopped onions
2	tablespoons chopped peeled fresh ginger
$2^1/_2$	cups $^1/_2$-inch cubes peeled butternut squash (from $1^1/_2$- to $1^3/_4$-pound squash)
2	medium-size white potatoes (about 11 ounces), peeled, cubed
$2^1/_2$	cups bottled clam juice
2	teaspoons curry powder
1	cup $^1/_2$-inch cubes zucchini
$^1/_4$	cup unsweetened coconut milk or whipping cream
1	pound bay scallops
	Chopped fresh cilantro

Melt butter in heavy large saucepan over medium-high heat. Add onions and ginger and sauté 2 minutes. Add squash, potatoes, clam juice and curry powder. Bring to boil. Reduce heat to medium-low, cover and simmer until potatoes are tender, about 15 minutes. Puree 2 cups of soup in blender. Return to pot. *(Can be made 1 day ahead. Refrigerate uncovered until cold, then cover and keep refrigerated.)*

Add zucchini and coconut milk to pot. Simmer soup uncovered until zucchini is just tender, about 5 minutes. Add scallops and simmer until just opaque in center, about 5 minutes. Season to taste with salt and pepper. Ladle chowder into bowls; sprinkle with cilantro and serve.

4 SERVINGS

Winter Supper for Four

Spinach Salad

Curried Scallop and
Vegetable Chowder
(at left)

Flatbread

Beer

Baked Pears with Currants
and Cinnamon
(page 167; halve recipe)

Grilled Eggplant and
Mozzarella Sandwiches

Nonstick vegetable oil spray gives the eggplant an even but light coat of oil that keeps it from sticking without adding too many calories. In fact, this entrée, including the salad, has just 202 calories per serving.

Nonstick vegetable oil spray
8   $1/2$-inch-thick eggplant slices
4   $1/4$-inch-thick slices part-skim mozzarella cheese (4 ounces)

2   tablespoons olive oil
$1^1/2$ tablespoons balsamic vinegar
1   garlic clove, minced
4   large bunches arugula
2   large tomatoes, coarsely chopped
3   tablespoons chopped fresh basil
2   tablespoons pine nuts, toasted

Spray grill with nonstick spray and prepare barbecue (medium heat). Spray eggplant on both sides with nonstick spray; sprinkle with salt and pepper. Grill until tender, turning occasionally, about 10 minutes. Place 1 cheese slice atop each of 4 eggplant slices; top with remaining eggplant slices. Grill until cheese melts, about 2 minutes longer.

Whisk oil, vinegar and garlic in large bowl. Season with salt and pepper. Add arugula, tomatoes and basil; toss. Divide among 4 plates. Sprinkle with pine nuts. Top each with 1 eggplant sandwich and serve.

4 SERVINGS

meatless

Polenta with Corn, Red Onion and Cucumber Salad

4 cups water

1 teaspoon salt

1 cup polenta (coarse cornmeal) or yellow cornmeal

$^1/_4$ cup grated Parmesan cheese

3 tablespoons fresh lime juice

2 tablespoons olive oil

1 garlic clove, minced

Nonstick vegetable oil spray

4 ears corn, husked

1 large red onion, cut into $^1/_2$-inch-thick slices

$2^1/_2$ cups chopped seeded tomatoes

$1^1/_4$ cups chopped English hothouse cucumber

$^1/_3$ cup chopped fresh mint

Begin this dish early in the day (or the night before) to allow the polenta enough time to set. If you're short on time, use a purchased polenta roll from the supermarket instead of making polenta at home. Slice the roll into $^1/_2$-inch-thick pieces, spray with nonstick vegetable oil spray and grill according to the recipe's instructions.

Bring 4 cups water and salt to boil in heavy large saucepan. Gradually add polenta, whisking until boiling and smooth. Reduce heat to low. Cook until very thick, whisking often, about 25 minutes (about 15 minutes for yellow cornmeal). Whisk in cheese. Spread in 8x8x2-inch glass baking dish. Cool slightly. Cover; chill at least 6 hours and up to 1 day.

Whisk lime juice, oil and garlic in large bowl to blend. Set dressing aside.

Spray grill with nonstick spray; prepare barbecue (medium heat). Spray corn and onion slices with nonstick spray. Sprinkle with salt and pepper. Grill vegetables until tender, turning often, about 8 minutes for corn and 15 minutes for onion. Cool. Cut corn kernels from cobs. Coarsely chop onion. Add corn, onion, tomatoes, cucumber and mint to dressing; toss to coat. Season salad to taste with salt and pepper.

Cut polenta into 4 squares. Cut each square diagonally into 2 triangles. Spray polenta with nonstick spray. Grill polenta until heated through, about 5 minutes per side.

Divide salad among 4 plates. Place 2 grilled polenta triangles alongside each salad and serve immediately.

4 SERVINGS

Two-Cheese Soufflé

Grated Parmesan cheese
1/4 cup (1/2 stick) butter
5 tablespoons all purpose flour
Pinch of cayenne pepper
Pinch of ground nutmeg
1 1/4 cups whole milk
1/4 cup dry white wine
6 large egg yolks
1 teaspoon salt
1/4 teaspoon ground black pepper
1 1/4 cups plus 2 tablespoons (packed) coarsely grated Gruyère cheese (about 6 ounces)
1/4 cup finely grated Parmesan cheese

8 large egg whites

After adding milk and white wine to the roux (a cooked combination of flour and butter), whisk the sauce constantly until it is smooth, thick and bubbling.

Fold coarsely grated Gruyère cheese and finely grated Parmesan cheese into the lukewarm sauce to make the soufflé base.

Beating the egg whites is an important step: The air that is whipped into them will expand in the oven and make the soufflé rise. Enough air has been beaten into the whites when they form stiff peaks but still look moist and billowy. (Overbeaten whites look dry and separated.)

Position rack in center of oven and preheat to 400°F. Generously butter one 10-cup soufflé dish or six 1 1/4-cup soufflé dishes; sprinkle with Parmesan cheese to coat. (If using 1 1/4-cup dishes, place all 6 on rimmed baking sheet.) Melt butter in heavy large saucepan over medium heat. Add flour, cayenne pepper and nutmeg. Cook without browning until mixture begins to bubble, whisking constantly, about 1 minute. Gradually whisk in milk, then wine. Cook until smooth, thick and beginning to boil, whisking constantly, about 2 minutes. Remove from heat. Mix yolks, salt and pepper in small bowl. Add yolk mixture all at once to sauce and whisk quickly to blend. Fold in 1 1/4 cups Gruyère cheese and 1/4 cup Parmesan cheese (cheeses do not need to melt).

Using electric mixer, beat egg whites in large bowl until stiff but not dry. Fold 1/4 of whites into lukewarm soufflé base to lighten. Fold in remaining whites. Transfer soufflé mixture to prepared dish. Sprinkle with remaining 2 tablespoons Gruyère cheese.

Place soufflé in oven; reduce heat to 375°F. Bake soufflé until puffed, golden and gently set in center, about 40 minutes for large soufflé (or 25 minutes for small soufflés). Using oven mitts, carefully transfer soufflé to platter and serve immediately.

4 TO 6 SERVINGS

Grilled Ratatouille Salad with Feta Cheese

1   12- to 14-ounce eggplant, cut into ¹/₂-inch-thick rounds
1   zucchini, quartered lengthwise
1   red bell pepper, cut lengthwise into 6 strips
1   medium onion, cut into ¹/₂-inch-thick rounds
3   tablespoons purchased garlic-flavored olive oil

2   to 3 teaspoons balsamic vinegar
²/₃ cup crumbled feta cheese
2   tablespoons slivered fresh basil

Prepare barbecue (medium-high heat). Place eggplant, zucchini, red bell pepper and onion on baking sheet. Drizzle with oil and sprinkle with salt and pepper; turn to coat. Grill vegetables until tender and tinged with brown, turning frequently, about 6 minutes for eggplant and zucchini and about 10 minutes for red bell pepper and onion.

Divide vegetables between 2 plates; drizzle with balsamic vinegar. Sprinkle feta cheese and slivered basil over and serve immediately.

2 SERVINGS

Greek-Style Vegetable Kebabs with Orzo and Feta

8   tablespoons purchased Greek-style vinaigrette
2   tablespoons minced fresh mint
¹/₂ cup orzo (rice-shaped pasta)

1   red bell pepper, cut into 1-inch cubes
3   Japanese eggplants, cut into ¹/₂-inch-thick rounds
2   medium zucchini, cut into ¹/₂-inch-thick rounds

¹/₂ cup crumbled feta cheese

Prepare barbecue (medium-high heat). Whisk vinaigrette and mint in small bowl to blend for dressing. Cook orzo in medium saucepan of boiling salted water until tender but still firm to bite; drain. Return orzo to same pan. Mix in 3 tablespoons dressing. Season with salt and pepper.

Thread bell pepper, eggplant and zucchini onto 4 metal skewers; brush with some of remaining dressing. Grill vegetables until tender and just charred, turning and brushing often with dressing, about 12 minutes.

Divide orzo between 2 plates. Place vegetable skewers atop orzo. Sprinkle with crumbled feta cheese and serve immediately.

2 SERVINGS

Portobello Burgers with Red Pepper Mayonnaise

$1/2$ cup chopped drained roasted red peppers from jar

$1/4$ cup low-fat mayonnaise

1 garlic clove, chopped

$1/8$ teaspoon cayenne pepper

Nonstick vegetable oil spray

4 large portobello mushrooms, stems removed

4 $1/2$-inch-thick red onion slices

4 $1/2$-inch-thick crusty country bread slices (each about 5x3 inches)

2 tablespoons rice vinegar

4 cups baby spinach leaves

Rich-tasting, hearty portobello mushrooms replace the meat in these open-face burgers. Serve them with fries or chips, if you like.

Blend red peppers, mayonnaise, garlic and cayenne pepper in processor until smooth. Season to taste with salt and pepper.

Spray grill with oil spray; prepare barbecue (medium heat). Spray mushrooms and onions with oil spray; sprinkle with salt and pepper. Grill vegetables and bread until vegetables are tender and bread is golden, turning often, 12 minutes for vegetables and 5 minutes for bread.

Transfer 2 tablespoons red pepper mayonnaise to large bowl. Whisk in vinegar; add spinach and toss. Divide among 4 plates. Place 1 bread slice atop spinach on each. Top each with 1 mushroom, then 1 onion slice. Spoon 2 tablespoons red pepper mayonnaise atop each and serve.

4 SERVINGS

Swiss Chard and Herb Tart

1 pound Swiss chard, stems and ribs removed

1¹/₂ tablespoons extra-virgin olive oil

1 garlic clove, minced

1 15-ounce container whole-milk ricotta cheese

¹/₂ cup freshly grated Parmesan cheese

2 large eggs

¹/₂ teaspoon salt

¹/₄ teaspoon ground black pepper

¹/₄ teaspoon minced fresh thyme

¹/₄ teaspoon minced fresh oregano

¹/₈ teaspoon grated nutmeg

1 17.3-ounce package frozen puff pastry (2 sheets), thawed

Cook chard in large pot of boiling salted water until just wilted, about 2 minutes. Drain. Squeeze out liquid. Chop chard.

Heat oil in heavy large skillet over medium heat. Add garlic; sauté 1 minute. Add chard; sauté until excess liquid evaporates, about 5 minutes. Transfer cooked chard mixture to large bowl. Cool slightly. Mix in ricotta cheese and next 7 ingredients.

Roll out 1 pastry sheet on lightly floured surface to 14-inch square. Transfer pastry to 9-inch-diameter tart pan with removable bottom. Trim edges, leaving 1-inch overhang. Fill pastry with chard mixture. Lightly brush pastry overhang with pastry brush dipped into water. Roll out second pastry sheet to 13-inch square. Using tart pan as guide, trim pastry square to 10-inch round. Drape over filling. Seal edges and fold in. *(Tart can be prepared up to 6 hours ahead. Cover and refrigerate.)*

Position rack in bottom third of oven; preheat to 375°F. Bake until pastry is golden brown, about 45 minutes (bake up to 1 hour if prepared ahead and refrigerated). Cool 10 minutes. Remove pan sides from tart. Transfer to platter. Cut into wedges and serve.

4 SERVINGS

Rustic Vegetarian Dinner for Four

Crispy Bruschetta with Goat Cheese, Tomatoes and Mint
(page 20)

Swiss Chard and Herb Tart
(at left; pictured opposite)

Roasted Root Vegetables with Balsamic Vinegar and Thyme
(page 126; halve recipe)

Chianti

Cherry Crumble Pie
(page 162)

Southwestern Tofu Wraps

Use your favorite variety of flavored tortillas (such as tomato or jalapeño) to add even more interest to these great wraps. Adjust the amount of heat by purchasing mild, medium or hot salsa to use in the wraps.

4 tablespoons fresh lime juice
1 tablespoon vegetable oil
8 ounces firm tofu, drained, patted dry, crumbled
$^1/_2$ cup chopped red onion
$^1/_3$ cup chopped fresh cilantro
1 garlic clove, minced
4 7- to 8-inch-diameter flour tortillas
2 cups thinly sliced lettuce leaves
1 cup spicy tomato salsa

Whisk 3 tablespoons lime juice and vegetable oil in medium bowl to blend. Add tofu, onion, cilantro and garlic and toss to blend. Season to taste with salt and pepper. Let marinate 20 minutes.

Preheat oven to 350°F. Wrap tortillas in foil. Place in oven until heated through, 10 minutes. Toss lettuce with 1 tablespoon lime juice in small bowl. Place 1 tortilla on each of 4 plates. Place lettuce down center of each tortilla. Top with tofu mixture, dividing equally. Spoon 1$^1/_2$ tablespoons salsa over each. Roll up and serve, passing remaining salsa separately.

4 SERVINGS

Fresh Corn Quiche

3 large eggs
$^1/_2$ small onion, coarsely chopped
1 tablespoon all purpose flour
1 tablespoon sugar
1 teaspoon salt
1$^1/_3$ cups half and half
3 tablespoons butter, melted
2 cups fresh corn kernels (cut from about 2 ears) or frozen, thawed
1 deep-dish frozen pie crust, thawed

Preheat oven to 375°F. Combine first 5 ingredients in processor; blend until onion is finely chopped. Add half and half and butter; process just until blended. Transfer to large bowl. Mix in corn. Pour into crust. Bake until filling is slightly puffed and top is golden, about 50 minutes. Transfer to rack; cool slightly. Serve warm.

6 SERVINGS

Gruyère Fondue with Caramelized Shallots

1 tablespoon butter

1¹/₄ cups thinly sliced shallots (about 6 ounces)

1 teaspoon sugar

1¹/₂ cups (or more) dry white wine

14 ounces grated Gruyère cheese (about 3¹/₂ cups packed)

2 tablespoons all purpose flour
Generous pinch of ground nutmeg

1 sourdough baguette, cut into 1-inch cubes

Melt butter in heavy medium skillet over medium heat. Add shallots and sauté 3 minutes. Reduce heat to low; sprinkle shallots with sugar, salt and pepper. Sauté shallots until caramelized, about 15 minutes. Transfer shallots to small bowl. Add 1¹/2 cups wine to skillet; boil 1 minute.

Pour wine into heavy medium saucepan; set over medium-low heat. Toss cheese with flour in medium bowl to coat. Add half of caramelized shallots to wine; add cheese mixture by handfuls, stirring until cheese melts and is smooth before adding more. Thin with more wine if mixture is too thick. Season with nutmeg, salt and pepper.

Transfer mixture to fondue pot. Set pot over candle or canned heat burner. Top fondue with remaining shallots. Serve with bread cubes.

4 SERVINGS

Fondue Options

Although the mellow, nutty-flavored Emmenthal is Switzerland's leading exported cheese, aficionados know that Gruyère (pronounced *grew-yair* or *gree-air*) is the one that gives a classic fondue its zing. Like Emmenthal, it has a nutty quality, but Gruyère has more complex flavors, its fruity and sweet overtones balanced by an appealing saltiness.

But Gruyère is not the only cheese well suited to fondue. Virtually any cheese that melts well can become the basis for the dish. Beaufort, Comté, Swiss Appenzeller, German Tilsit, French Camembert and Italian Fontina are all good choices.

The other ingredients that add character to fondue are also variable. Many classic recipes add a splash of cherry-flavored kirsch to the dry white wine used; other fruit-flavored brandies such as Calvados, made from apples, would work well instead. In place of the shallots used in the recipe at left, try using garlic. To add a more subtle garlic flavor, simply rub the inside of the pot with the cut side of a single clove before other ingredients are added. Dried mushrooms, reconstituted in water or wine, and shaved white truffles make particularly aromatic embellishments.

pasta & pizza

Pasta with Sausage, Eggplant and Basil

1	large eggplant, cut into 1-inch pieces
1	tablespoon salt
7	tablespoons olive oil
1³/₄	pounds hot Italian sausages, casings removed, meat shaped into 1¹/₄-inch meatballs (about 46)
1	pound cherry tomatoes, halved
6	garlic cloves, finely chopped
1¹/₂	serrano chilies, seeded, finely chopped (about 1 tablespoon)
1¹/₄	cups canned low-salt chicken broth
²/₃	cup whipping cream
1	pound cavatapi or penne pasta
1	cup freshly grated Parmesan cheese
1	cup (lightly packed) fresh basil leaves, torn into ¹/₂-inch pieces
²/₃	cup pine nuts, toasted
	Additional grated Parmesan cheese

Toss eggplant with 1 tablespoon salt in large colander. Place colander over large bowl and let stand 30 minutes.

Heat 3 tablespoons oil in heavy large skillet over medium-high heat. Working in batches, add eggplant; sauté until golden, about 5 minutes. Transfer to medium bowl. *(Can be made 8 hours ahead. Cover; chill.)*

Heat 2 tablespoons oil in heavy large skillet over medium-high heat. Working in batches, cook meatballs until brown, about 5 minutes. Transfer meatballs to paper-towel-lined plate. Wipe out skillet. Heat remaining 2 tablespoons oil in same skillet over medium-high heat. Add tomatoes, garlic and chilies; sauté until fragrant, about 2 minutes. Add meatballs, broth and cream. Simmer until meatballs are cooked through, about 5 minutes. Add eggplant and simmer 1 minute.

Meanwhile, cook pasta in large pot of boiling salted water until tender but still firm to bite. Drain. Transfer to large bowl.

Toss pasta with sauce and 1 cup Parmesan cheese. Mix in basil and pine nuts. Season to taste with salt and pepper. Serve pasta, passing additional grated Parmesan cheese separately.

8 SERVINGS

Linguine with Shellfish Sauce

A shellfish lover's dream, this flavorful sauce includes six kinds. If you can't get them all, substitute according to what's freshest and best at the local market.

6 tablespoons extra-virgin olive oil

2 garlic cloves, minced

³/₄ teaspoon dried crushed red pepper

12 ounces cleaned squid, bodies cut into ¹/₂-inch-wide rings, tentacles left whole

1¹/₄ cups dry white wine

1 28-ounce can Italian-style tomatoes with basil

2 teaspoons tomato paste

¹/₄ cup water

2 pounds small littleneck clams, scrubbed

1 pound mussels, scrubbed, debearded

1 10-ounce uncooked lobster tail, shelled, meat cut into 1-inch pieces

8 ounces uncooked large shrimp, peeled, deveined

4 ounces bay scallops

3 tablespoons chopped fresh Italian parsley

1 pound linguine

Heat 3 tablespoons oil in large skillet over medium heat. Add garlic and dried red pepper; stir 1 minute. Add squid; sauté just until opaque, about 3 minutes. Add wine; simmer until liquid is reduced by half, about 20 minutes. Add tomatoes with juices and tomato paste. Bring to simmer, breaking up tomatoes. Cover; simmer over low heat 40 minutes.

Bring ¹/₄ cup water to boil in another large skillet over high heat. Add clams and mussels. Cover; cook until shells open, about 6 minutes (discard any clams and mussels that do not open). Transfer shellfish to colander set over medium bowl and drain well.

Strain juices from skillet and medium bowl through fine sieve into tomato sauce. Simmer sauce uncovered until slightly thickened, about 10 minutes. Add lobster, shrimp and scallops. Simmer 2 minutes. Add clams and mussels from colander. Simmer 1 minute longer. Stir in remaining 3 tablespoons oil and parsley. Season with salt and pepper.

Meanwhile, cook linguine in pot of boiling salted water until tender but still firm to bite. Drain. Return to pot. Add shellfish sauce; toss to coat.

4 TO 6 SERVINGS

Baked Penne with Eggplant, Olives and Feta Cheese

8 tablespoons olive oil

$3/4$ pound red bell peppers, diced

6 large garlic cloves, chopped

$1/2$ teaspoon dried crushed red pepper

1 $1^{1}/4$-pound eggplant, unpeeled, cut into $1/2$-inch cubes

1 tablespoon dried leaf oregano

1 28-ounce can diced tomatoes in juice

1 cup thinly sliced fresh basil

$1/2$ cup coarsely chopped pitted Kalamata olives or other brine-cured black olives

$1/4$ cup tomato paste

2 tablespoons red wine vinegar

12 ounces penne pasta

14 ounces feta cheese, crumbled

Brush 13x9x2-inch glass baking dish with 2 tablespoons oil. Heat remaining 6 tablespoons oil in heavy large pot over medium-high heat. Add bell peppers, garlic and dried red pepper; sauté 3 minutes. Add eggplant and oregano. Reduce heat to medium-low. Cover; cook until eggplant softens, stirring often, about 15 minutes. Mix in tomatoes with juices, $1/2$ cup basil, olives, tomato paste and vinegar. Cover; simmer until all vegetables are tender, stirring occasionally, about 12 minutes. Season to taste with salt and pepper.

Cook pasta in large pot of boiling salted water until tender but still firm to bite; drain. Stir pasta into vegetable mixture. Transfer to prepared dish and cover with foil. *(Can be prepared 1 day ahead. Refrigerate.)*

Preheat oven to 350°F. Bake pasta covered until heated through, about 20 minutes (40 minutes if chilled). Sprinkle with feta, then $1/2$ cup basil.

8 TO 10 SERVINGS

Feta cheese and black olives lend Greek flavor to this baked pasta dish. And like most pasta casseroles, it's handy from the do-ahead perspective: Make it a day in advance and bake just before serving.

The tortelli can be made up to two weeks ahead and frozen. Dust them lightly with flour and then wrap in foil. They do not need to be defrosted before cooking.

POTATO-SAUSAGE FILLING

10	to 11 ounces small white-skinned potatoes (about 3), unpeeled
1	sweet Italian sausage
$1/2$	cup freshly grated Parmesan cheese
$1/3$	cup chopped fresh Italian parsley
1	large egg
1	garlic clove, minced
$1/2$	teaspoon salt
$1/4$	teaspoon ground black pepper
$1/8$	teaspoon ground nutmeg

BASIC EGG PASTA DOUGH

3	cups all purpose flour
4	large eggs
1	tablespoon olive oil
$1/2$	teaspoon salt
$1/2$	cup (1 stick) butter
	Ragù (see recipe opposite)
	Freshly grated Parmesan cheese

FOR FILLING: Bring large pot of salted water to boil. Add potatoes and sausage; boil until sausage is cooked through, 10 minutes. Transfer sausage to plate. Continue to cook potatoes until tender, 15 minutes. Drain well. Peel potatoes; place in large bowl. Using hand masher, mash potatoes to smooth paste. Mix in cheese, then next 6 ingredients. Finely chop sausage; mix in. Cover; set filling aside up to 1 hour.

FOR PASTA DOUGH: Mound flour on work surface. Make large shallow well (about 5 inches in diameter) in center. Add eggs, oil and salt to well. Using fork, whisk eggs, oil and salt to blend. Gradually work in enough flour from around egg mixture to form soft dough in center of flour ring (there will be flour left over). Gather dough into ball. Knead dough on work surface until smooth and elastic, working in more flour if sticky, about 10 minutes. Cover with plastic; let rest 45 minutes.

Line 2 large baking sheets with parchment paper. Cut dough into 4 pieces.

Turn pasta machine to widest setting. Flatten 1 dough piece into rectangle. Cover remaining pieces with plastic. Run dough through machine 3 times. Fold uneven ends over to make straight edge. Run through machine 2 more times, dusting with flour if sticky. Adjust machine to next narrower setting. Run dough through machine 3 times. Cut dough strip in half crosswise for easier handling. Working with half of dough strip and keeping other half covered with plastic to prevent drying, repeat running dough through machine 3 times on each narrower setting until pasta is ¹/₁₆ inch thick, dusting with flour very lightly if sticky (each dough strip will be about 20 inches long and 4 inches wide).

Place 1 dough strip on work surface. Starting ³/₄ inch in from 1 short side, drop filling by heaping teaspoonfuls along 1 long side of strip, spacing 1 inch apart and about ¹/₂ inch in from edge. Fold opposite long side of dough over mounds of filling. Press around mounds of filling to release any air, then press dough between mounds to seal. Press edges together to seal. Cut dough between mounds of filling into individual tortelli. Transfer to prepared sheets. Repeat with second dough strip.

Repeat rolling out reserved dough pieces into 2 strips, then filling and shaping into tortelli until all filling is used. Discard remaining dough.

Cook tortelli in large pot of boiling salted water until tender, about 5 minutes (6 minutes if frozen). Drain. Add butter to same pot; melt over medium-high heat. Add tortelli; toss gently until warm and coated with butter. Meanwhile, bring Ragù to simmer. Divide tortelli among plates. Drizzle with butter from pot. Top with Ragù; sprinkle with cheese. Garnish with parsley. Serve with more cheese and any remaining Ragù.

4 SERVINGS

Begin making the dough by mounding three cups of flour on the work surface. Then clear out the center to create a large, shallow well for the eggs, oil and salt.

Use a fork to beat the egg mixture before adding flour, little by little, from around the well.

Ragù

- ¹/₄ cup extra-virgin olive oil
- 3 sweet Italian sausages, casings removed
- 1 cup chopped celery
- ³/₄ cup chopped carrot
- ³/₄ cup chopped red onion
- 2 tablespoons chopped fresh Italian parsley
- 1 large garlic clove, minced
  Large pinch of dried crushed red pepper
- 2 cups chicken stock or canned low-salt chicken broth
- ³/₄ cup tomato paste

Heat oil in large pot over medium-high heat. Add sausage and sauté until no longer pink, breaking up with back of fork, about 2 minutes. Add celery, carrot, onion, parsley, garlic and red pepper. Sauté until vegetables begin to soften, about 5 minutes. Add stock and tomato paste. Reduce heat to medium-low and simmer until ragù thickens slightly, stirring occasionally, about 20 minutes. Season with salt and pepper.

MAKES 3 CUPS

Incorporate enough flour to form pasta dough that is soft and still a bit sticky.

Perfect Pasta Every Time

Follow these tips for cooking a pound of pasta perfectly—every time.

- Bring four to six quarts of cold water to a rolling boil in a large pot; add two tablespoons of salt.
- Add pasta to boiling salted water. Stir pasta with a wooden spoon occasionally to prevent sticking.
- Begin testing pasta at the earliest point you think it might be *al dente*—tender but still somewhat chewy and slightly resistant when bitten. Cooking time usually ranges from seven to fourteen minutes for dried purchased pasta.
- Drain briefly (do not rinse), reserving about one cup of the starchy pasta cooking water.
- Return drained pasta to pot. Add sauce and toss to combine. Pasta should be evenly coated, with no excess sauce left in the pot.
- Add some of reserved pasta cooking water by tablespoonfuls if sauce is too thick; toss to combine. The starchy water will also lend a creamy quality to pasta dishes.
- Serve pasta immediately, in warmed bowls if desired.

Fettuccine with Porcini Sauce

1/4	cup (1/2 stick) butter
4	large shallots, chopped
1	ounce dried porcini mushrooms, rinsed if sandy
2	cups canned low-salt chicken broth
1	cup whipping cream
12	ounces fettuccine
	Grated Parmesan cheese

Melt butter in skillet over medium-high heat. Add shallots; sauté until just brown, 4 minutes. Stir in mushrooms. Add broth and cream; bring to boil. Reduce heat to medium-low, cover and simmer until mushrooms are tender, 20 minutes. Uncover; boil until slightly thickened, stirring, 5 minutes.

Cook pasta in large pot of boiling salted water until tender but still firm to bite. Drain, reserving 1/2 cup cooking water. Return pasta to pot. Add sauce; toss over medium-low heat until heated through, adding cooking water by tablespoonfuls if pasta is dry. Serve, passing cheese separately.

4 TO 6 SERVINGS

Noodles with Bok Choy and Tofu

1/4	cup soy sauce
2	tablespoons balsamic vinegar
2	tablespoons honey
2	tablespoons oriental sesame oil
2	teaspoons cornstarch
8	green onions, chopped
2	large garlic cloves, minced
1	tablespoon minced peeled fresh ginger
2	heads bok choy, bottom third discarded, leaves thickly sliced
1	12-ounce package extra-firm tofu, cut into 1/2-inch pieces, drained well
1	12-ounce package udon noodles or 12 ounces linguine, freshly cooked

Whisk soy sauce, vinegar, honey, 1 tablespoon oil and cornstarch in small bowl to blend. Heat remaining oil in heavy large pot over medium-high heat. Add onions, garlic and ginger and stir 30 seconds. Add bok choy and sauté until beginning to wilt, about 2 minutes. Mix in tofu, then noodles and soy mixture. Stir until sauce thickens, about 1 minute.

4 SERVINGS

Spinach and Ricotta Gnocchi

4 6-ounce packages ready-to-use baby spinach leaves

2 cups whole-milk ricotta cheese (about 16 ounces)

1 cup freshly grated Parmesan cheese

$^1/_2$ cup (about) all purpose flour

2 large egg yolks

$^1/_2$ teaspoon salt

$^1/_2$ teaspoon ground black pepper

Generous pinch of ground nutmeg

$^1/_4$ cup ($^1/_2$ stick) butter, melted

Cook spinach in large pot of boiling salted water just until wilted, stirring occasionally, about 2 minutes. Drain. Squeeze out liquid. Chop spinach.

Mix spinach, ricotta, $^1/_2$ cup Parmesan, $^1/_2$ cup flour, egg yolks, salt, pepper and nutmeg in bowl until slightly sticky dough forms.

Dust baking sheet with flour. Working in batches and using floured hands, roll $^1/_4$ cup dough on floured work surface to form 5-inch-long rope. Cut rope into 1-inch pieces. Roll each piece between palms to form oval. Transfer gnocchi to prepared baking sheet. Repeat rolling, cutting and shaping with remaining dough.

Working in batches, add gnocchi to pot of boiling salted water; cook until gnocchi rise to surface. Cook 4 minutes longer. Using slotted spoon, remove gnocchi from water; drain. Place in serving dish.

Pour butter over gnocchi and toss to coat. *(Can be made 1 day ahead. Cover; chill. Reheat in 400°F oven about 10 minutes.)* Sprinkle gnocchi with remaining $^1/_2$ cup Parmesan. Season to taste with salt and pepper.

4 SERVINGS

Gnocchi means "dumplings" in Italian; this version of pasta dumplings includes ricotta cheese and spinach in the dough. Make the gnocchi and cook them a day ahead; reheat just before serving.

Artichoke and Feta Cheese Pizza

Refrigerated pizza crust dough makes this quick and easy to prepare. Sliced fresh mint gives it wonderful flavor.

1   6.5-ounce jar marinated artichoke hearts, drained, 2 tablespoons marinade reserved
1   tablespoon yellow cornmeal
1   10-ounce tube refrigerated pizza crust dough
6   ounces plum tomatoes, thinly sliced into rounds
1   cup crumbled herb-seasoned feta cheese (about 4 ounces)
½   medium-size sweet onion (such as Vidalia or Maui), thinly sliced
2   tablespoons thinly sliced fresh mint

Preheat oven to 425°F. Cut artichokes into ½-inch pieces. Sprinkle baking sheet with yellow cornmeal. Unroll pizza crust dough onto prepared baking sheet; press out dough to 11-inch square. Brush dough with 1 tablespoon reserved marinade. Top dough with artichokes, plum tomato slices, crumbled herb-seasoned feta cheese and sweet onion slices. Drizzle with remaining 1 tablespoon marinade.

Bake pizza until crust is crisp and golden, about 15 minutes. Transfer to platter. Sprinkle with mint. Cut pizza into 4 squares and serve.

2 SERVINGS

Wild Mushroom Pizza with Garlic Confit and Bacon

    3   bacon slices, cut crosswise into $1/2$-inch pieces
    2   tablespoons olive oil
  $1/2$ cup halved peeled large garlic cloves (about $2^{1}/_{2}$ ounces)
   12   ounces assorted fresh wild mushrooms, thinly sliced
  $1/2$ red bell pepper, cut into matchstick-size strips

    1   10-ounce purchased fully baked thin pizza crust
    1   cup (packed) mixed shredded Italian cheeses (about 4 ounces)

Cook bacon in large skillet over medium heat until golden, about 10 minutes. Using slotted spoon, transfer bacon to paper towels. Pour off drippings from skillet. Add oil and garlic to skillet. Cover and cook over low heat until garlic is golden, stirring occasionally, about 15 minutes. Add mushrooms and bell pepper; cover and cook over high heat until vegetables are tender, stirring often, about 5 minutes. Season to taste with salt and pepper. *(Can be made 8 hours ahead; chill bacon and vegetables separately.)*

Preheat oven to 450°F. Place pizza crust on baking sheet. Sprinkle cheeses, then vegetable mixture and bacon over crust. Bake until cheeses melt, about 15 minutes. Remove from oven. Let stand 2 minutes. Cut pizza into wedges and serve immediately.

2 SERVINGS

Mushroom Prep 101

Unlike most vegetables, mushrooms don't benefit from a dunking in clean sink water. Don't submerge mushrooms in water: They are very porous; when washed, they absorb water and can become soggy and difficult to brown. Instead, simply trim the stems, and use a pastry brush or a damp paper towel to remove any dirt.

Morels require a more thorough cleansing because their crevices can collect dirt. Rinse them in a bowl of water and drain well before using. The stems of fresh shiitake and portobello mushrooms are tough and should be completely cut away; they can, however, be used to flavor a stock and then discarded, if desired.

It isn't necessary to remove the gills of most cultivated and wild mushrooms. Portobellos are the exception—when the mushrooms are used whole, the gills can remain intact, but if the mushrooms are going to be chopped, scoop out the gills first because they can discolor other ingredients in a dish.

Radicchio, Grapefruit and Spinach Salad
(page 143)

On the Side

side dishes

salads

breads

Mashed Potatoes, Pears and Leeks

Pears are the unusual ingredient in this side dish; their texture combines well with the potatoes, and they add a touch of sweetness. Note that the recipe can be made a day ahead, and then rewarmed just before serving.

3¹/₂ pounds Yukon Gold potatoes, peeled, cut into ¹/₂-inch cubes
2 pounds ripe pears, peeled, cored, cut into ¹/₂-inch cubes
8 tablespoons (1 stick) margarine or butter, room temperature
2 cups sliced leeks (white and pale green parts only; about 2 large)

Brush 13x9x2-inch glass baking dish with margarine. Steam half of potatoes and pears until very tender, about 15 minutes. Transfer to large bowl; cover to keep warm. Repeat steaming with remaining potatoes and pears. Empty pot. Return all potatoes and pears to pot. Add 6 tablespoons margarine; mash mixture well. Season with salt and pepper.

Melt 2 tablespoons margarine in large skillet. Add leeks; sauté until crisp-tender, about 5 minutes. Mix half of leeks into potato mixture; transfer to prepared dish. Top with remaining leeks. *(Can be made 1 day ahead. Cover; chill. Rewarm uncovered in 350°F oven 25 minutes.)*

8 SERVINGS

Roasted Root Vegetables with Balsamic Vinegar and Thyme

side dishes

4 large beets, peeled, cut into ³/₄-inch-thick wedges
2 pounds turnips, peeled, cut into ³/₄-inch-thick wedges
2 pounds large red-skinned potatoes, peeled, cut into ³/₄-inch-thick wedges
2 pounds red onions, peeled, cut into ³/₄-inch-thick wedges with some core still attached
1¹/₂ pounds carrots, peeled, cut into ³/₄-inch-thick pieces
1¹/₄ pounds rutabagas, peeled, cut into ³/₄-inch-thick wedges
10 tablespoons olive oil
5 tablespoons balsamic vinegar
3 tablespoons chopped fresh thyme

Additional olive oil

Place vegetables in very large bowl. Add oil, 3 tablespoons vinegar and thyme; toss to coat. Sprinkle with salt and pepper.

Place oven racks in top third and bottom third of oven; preheat to 400°F. Brush 2 large baking sheets with oil. Divide vegetables between sheets. Roast vegetables until tender, stirring occasionally, about 1 hour.

A mix of beets, turnips, potatoes, red onions, carrots and rutabagas is enlivened with balsamic vinegar in this do-ahead side dish.

Drizzle remaining 2 tablespoons vinegar over. Season to taste with salt and pepper. *(Can be made 2 hours ahead. Let stand at room temperature. Rewarm in 400°F oven 20 minutes.)*

8 SERVINGS

Sugar Snap Peas with Toasted Sesame Seeds

1 pound sugar snap peas, stringed
1 teaspoon toasted sesame seeds
1 teaspoon oriental sesame oil

Steam sugar snap peas until crisp-tender, about 3 minutes. Transfer to bowl. Toss with sesame seeds and oil. Season to taste with salt.

6 SERVINGS

Garlic Mashed Potatoes with Corn

Corn adds texture and saffron threads add color and flavor to these special mashed potatoes. Serve them alongside any grilled meat or poultry.

1¹/₂ tablespoons olive oil
³/₄ cup chopped onion
1 cup fresh corn kernels
3 garlic cloves, minced
³/₄ cup whipping cream
2 tablespoons (¹/₄ stick) butter
¹/₄ teaspoon saffron threads

1³/₄ pounds russet potatoes, peeled, cut into 1-inch pieces

Heat oil in heavy medium skillet over medium heat. Add onion; sauté 5 minutes. Add corn and garlic; sauté until onion is golden and corn is tender, about 5 minutes longer. Add cream, butter and saffron. Bring to boil. Remove from heat. Cover and let stand 20 minutes.

Meanwhile, cook potatoes in large pot of boiling salted water until tender, about 20 minutes. Drain well. Transfer to large bowl. Mash until smooth. Stir in corn mixture. Season to taste with salt and pepper.

4 SERVINGS

Lentils with Port-glazed Shallots

1¹/₂ cups ruby Port
8 ounces small shallots plus 1 large shallot, peeled

1¹/₂ cups dried lentils (about 12 ounces), rinsed, drained
3 cups water

1 tablespoon olive oil

Combine Port and small shallots in heavy medium saucepan. Simmer over medium heat until shallots are tender and Port glazes shallots, stirring occasionally, about 35 minutes. Set aside. *(Port-glazed shallots can be prepared 8 hours ahead. Keep at room temperature.)*

Finely chop large shallot. Combine chopped shallot, lentils and 3 cups water in large saucepan. Bring to boil. Reduce heat to medium-low. Cover and simmer until lentils are just tender, about 30 minutes.

Rewarm Port mixture over medium-low heat. Stir oil and Port mixture into lentils. Season with salt and pepper. Transfer to bowl and serve.

4 SERVINGS

Jasmine Rice Timbales with Sesame Seeds

1½ cups jasmine rice or long-grain white rice
2 tablespoons (¼ stick) butter
3 teaspoons oriental sesame oil
2½ cups water
¼ teaspoon salt

¼ cup finely chopped chives
2 tablespoons white sesame seeds, toasted
1 tablespoon black sesame seeds

Combine rice, 1 tablespoon butter, 1 teaspoon sesame oil, 2½ cups water and ¼ teaspoon salt in large saucepan. Bring to boil. Reduce heat to low. Cover and simmer until rice is tender, stirring once, about 15 minutes.

Add remaining 1 tablespoon butter, chives and white and black sesame seeds to rice. Fluff with fork. Cover and let stand 5 minutes. Fluff rice again. Season to taste with salt and pepper.

Brush six ¾-cup soufflé dishes or custard cups with remaining 2 teaspoons sesame oil. Divide rice among dishes. Pack rice tightly into dishes. Turn timbales out onto plates and serve.

6 SERVINGS

Spinach, Basil and Ricotta Puree

2 cups water
2 10-ounce packages fresh spinach leaves
¾ cup fresh basil leaves
¾ cup whole-milk ricotta cheese
2 tablespoons (¼ stick) butter
1 garlic clove, minced
¼ cup whipping cream

Bring 2 cups water to boil in large pot. Add spinach and stir until tender and bright green, about 3 minutes. Drain. Squeeze out excess water. Transfer spinach to processor. Add basil and ricotta. Blend until smooth.

Melt butter in medium saucepan over medium heat. Add garlic; sauté until golden, about 3 minutes. Add spinach mixture and cream. Stir until just heated through. Season with salt and pepper. Transfer to bowl; serve.

4 SERVINGS

The Right Rice

Rice is rice, right? Actually, there are more than seven thousand varieties grown around the world. The trick is to pick the right rice for a particular recipe. Fortunately, the types available commercially may be organized into a few distinct categories.

Long-grain rices have slender grains that are four to five times longer than they are wide. When cooked, they form fairly dry, separate grains, which make ideal pilafs. Some long-grain varieties, such as Indian basmati rice and Asian jasmine rice, are particularly aromatic.

Medium-grain rices are shorter and plumper. After cooking, they tend to clump together as they cool. They are good all-purpose varieties.

Short-grain rices range from being about twice as long as they are wide to almost spherical. Rich in starch, they become sticky when cooked. That quality makes such short-grain rices as Japanese *mochi* or Italian *arborio* ideal choices for sushi and risotto, respectively.

All rices may also be categorized as brown or white. Brown rice has its bran coating and germ intact, giving it an earthy flavor and chewy texture. White rice has had that coating and germ milled away, leaving it milder in taste and slightly softer in texture.

Artichokes Stuffed with Pancetta and Parsley

Pancetta and parsley make a delicious filling for these artichokes. Don't discard the stems—they are sliced, cooked and served alongside the whole artichokes.

2 lemons, halved

4 large artichokes

3 tablespoons olive oil

3 ounces pancetta,* finely chopped

1/2 cup minced fresh Italian parsley

2/3 cup water

Squeeze juice from 1 lemon into large bowl of cold water; add 2 squeezed lemon halves. Cut stem off 1 artichoke; cut stem into 1/4-inch-thick rounds. Place rounds in lemon water. Starting at base of artichoke, bend outer leaves back; snap off where leaves break naturally, leaving tender yellow-green leaves attached. Using vegetable peeler, trim outside of base until no dark green areas remain. Rub cut surfaces with remaining lemon halves. Cut off top half of artichoke. Pull out purple-tipped leaves from center of artichoke. Using spoon, scoop out fibrous choke. Place artichoke in lemon water. Repeat with remaining artichokes.

Drain artichokes and stems. Heat 2 tablespoons olive oil in heavy large skillet over medium heat. Add artichokes and artichoke stem rounds. Cook until artichokes are golden, about 4 minutes per side. Remove from heat. Transfer stem rounds to small bowl.

Mix pancetta and parsley in bowl; spoon into artichokes. Drizzle 1 tablespoon oil over artichokes in skillet. Add ⅔ cup water; bring to boil. Cover; cook artichokes over medium-low heat until cooking liquid is reduced by about half, about 25 minutes. Add stem rounds; cook about 2 minutes. Serve artichokes surrounded by stem rounds and cooking liquid.

Pancetta, Italian bacon cured in salt, is available at Italian markets and also at some specialty foods stores across the country.

4 SERVINGS

Bacon and Molasses Beans

4	thick-cut bacon slices, thinly sliced crosswise
2	medium onions, finely chopped
¹/₂	green bell pepper, finely chopped
2	garlic cloves, minced
4	15-ounce cans Great Northern beans, rinsed, drained
¹/₃	cup mild-flavored (light) molasses
¹/₄	cup ketchup
¹/₄	cup purchased barbecue sauce
1	tablespoon Worcestershire sauce
1	tablespoon Dijon mustard
1	tablespoon apple cider vinegar

Chunks of bacon and molasses give this classic summer side dish extra richness and flavor. Purchased barbecue sauce cuts down on preparation time.

Cook bacon in heavy large pot over medium heat until crisp, about 5 minutes. Using slotted spoon, transfer bacon to paper towels; drain. Discard all but 2 tablespoons drippings in pot. Add onions, bell pepper and garlic to pot; sauté until vegetables are tender, about 8 minutes. Stir in bacon, beans and remaining ingredients. Reduce heat to medium-low; simmer uncovered until mixture thickens, stirring occasionally, about 10 minutes. Season with salt and pepper. *(Can be made 1 day ahead. Cover and refrigerate. Rewarm over medium heat, stirring often, about 10 minutes.)*

6 SERVINGS

Indian Ratatouille

Ratatouille, a vegetable stew native to France, always has eggplant, zucchini, tomatoes, onions, garlic and herbs in it; this version gets its Indian taste from the addition of fresh ginger, mustard seeds and a jalapeño chili.

1/4 cup vegetable oil
1 tablespoon mustard seeds
1 8-ounce red onion, cut into 1/2-inch pieces
1 large jalapeño chili, chopped
1 tablespoon chopped peeled fresh ginger
2 3/4-pound eggplants, quartered lengthwise, cut crosswise into 1/3-inch-thick slices
2 medium zucchini, halved lengthwise, cut crosswise into 1/3-inch-thick slices
3/4 pound plum tomatoes, chopped
3 large garlic cloves, chopped
2 tablespoons chopped fresh mint
1 tablespoon fresh lemon juice

Heat oil in heavy large pot over medium-high heat. Add mustard seeds; cook until seeds darken and begin to pop, about 2 minutes. Add onion, chili and ginger; stir 1 minute. Add eggplant and zucchini slices; stir 5 minutes. Cover; cook 5 minutes. Mix in tomatoes and garlic. Reduce heat to medium. Cover and cook until vegetables are tender, stirring occasionally, about 25 minutes. Mix in mint and lemon juice. Season to taste with salt and pepper and serve.

6 SERVINGS

Baked Potato Wedges with Seasoned Salt

8 large russet potatoes, peeled
1/2 cup (1 stick) butter, melted
1/2 cup olive oil
2 tablespoons seasoned salt

Preheat oven to 450°F. Cut each potato lengthwise into 8 wedges; toss in bowl with butter, oil and seasoned salt. Arrange in single layer on 2 baking sheets. Bake until tender and golden, turning potatoes and rotating sheets halfway through baking, about 45 minutes. Serve immediately.

10 SERVINGS

White Beans with Sage and Olive Oil

1 pound dried Great Northern beans

6 cups cold water

$^1/_4$ cup extra-virgin olive oil

$1^1/_2$ tablespoons chopped fresh sage

1 large garlic clove, minced

Additional olive oil

Note that the beans need to soak in water overnight, so get started at least one day before you plan to serve this side dish.

Place Great Northern beans in heavy large saucepan. Add enough cold water to cover beans by 3 inches and let soak overnight.

Drain beans and return to pan. Add 6 cups cold water, $^1/_4$ cup oil, chopped sage and garlic. Bring to boil. Reduce heat to medium-low. Cover partially; simmer until beans are just tender, stirring occasionally, about 45 minutes. Season with salt and pepper. *(Can be made 1 day ahead. Cool. Cover and keep chilled. Rewarm before continuing.)*

Using slotted spoon, transfer beans to bowl. Top with more oil.

6 SERVINGS

Skillet Potatoes with Red Onion and Chives

2 pounds small red-skinned new potatoes, unpeeled

5 tablespoons olive oil

1 cup coarsely chopped red onion

1/4 cup chopped fresh chives

Cook potatoes in large pot of boiling salted water until almost tender, about 15 minutes. Drain well. Cover and chill until cold, at least 3 hours or overnight. Cut potatoes into 1/2- to 3/4-inch pieces.

Heat oil in large skillet over medium-high heat. Add potatoes and red onion and sauté until potatoes are brown and crisp, stirring occasionally, about 35 minutes. Season to taste with salt and pepper. Transfer potato mixture to serving dish. Sprinkle with chives.

6 SERVINGS

Saffron Couscous with Fresh Peas and Chives

1   14^1/$_2$-ounce can low-salt chicken broth
1^1/$_2$ cups shelled fresh peas or frozen peas
2   tablespoons (^{1}/$_4$ stick) butter
      Pinch of saffron threads
1^1/$_4$ cups couscous
^{1}/$_4$ cup chopped fresh chives

Bring chicken broth to simmer in medium saucepan. Add peas and cook just until tender, about 2 minutes. Using slotted spoon, transfer peas to bowl. Add 2 tablespoons butter and saffron threads to broth and bring to boil. Remove from heat. Add couscous; stir to blend. Cover tightly and let stand until liquid is absorbed and couscous is tender, about 5 minutes. Fluff couscous with fork. Gently mix in chives and peas. Season to taste with salt and pepper. Transfer couscous to large bowl.

4 SERVINGS

Grilled Asparagus with Aioli

^{1}/$_4$ cup red wine vinegar
1   tablespoon honey
      Large pinch of saffron threads
1   cup mayonnaise
2   garlic cloves, minced
2   pounds asparagus, trimmed
3   tablespoons olive oil
1   small red bell pepper, finely chopped

Whisk vinegar, honey and saffron threads in heavy small saucepan over medium-high heat. Bring to boil. Remove from heat. Cool completely. Mix mayonnaise and garlic in medium bowl to blend. Mix in cooled vinegar mixture. Season aioli to taste with salt and pepper. *(Aioli can be prepared 1 day ahead. Cover with plastic and refrigerate.)*

Prepare barbecue (medium-high heat). Toss asparagus with olive oil on rimmed baking sheet. Sprinkle with salt and pepper. Grill asparagus until crisp-tender, turning occasionally, about 5 minutes. Transfer to platter. Drizzle aioli over asparagus. Sprinkle with red bell pepper and serve.

6 SERVINGS

- Saffron: Almost a quarter-million dried hand-picked stigmas from a particular type of crocus flower are needed to produce one pound of this rare spice. A pinch of saffron contributes brilliant golden color and aromatic flavor to rice dishes such as Spanish paella; it's also used in sauces, baked goods and even desserts. Buy saffron threads (the whole dried stigmas); ground saffron loses its power more quickly, and could be adulterated with less expensive ingredients such as turmeric.
- Truffles: Found underground near the roots of oak trees and hunted by specially trained dogs or pigs, these knobby fungi have an intensely aromatic flavor. Earthy-tasting black truffles come primarily from southwestern France and Umbria in central Italy; more pungent, slightly garlicky white truffles are found mostly in Northern Italy's Piedmont region. Use minced, peeled, cooked black truffles to flavor sauces for meat, poultry or game, and in egg dishes or very elegant mashed potatoes. Shave raw white truffles over pasta, risotto or polenta just before serving. Refrigerate whole fresh truffles for no more than a few days, buried in a bowl of whole eggs or in a covered jar of uncooked rice; their aroma will permeate those ingredients, yielding truffle-flavored dishes in which no truffles actually appear.

Down-East Succotash

The classic New England side dish of corn, beans and salt pork is updated and simplified for modern tastes.

5 bacon slices, coarsely chopped
2 shallots, chopped
2 10-ounce packages frozen corn kernels, thawed
2 10-ounce packages frozen large lima beans, thawed
$3/4$ cup canned low-salt chicken broth
2 teaspoons chopped fresh tarragon
1 1-pint basket cherry tomatoes, halved

Cook bacon in large skillet over medium heat until crisp and brown. Using slotted spoon, transfer bacon to paper towels to drain. Pour off all but 3 tablespoons fat from skillet. Return skillet to medium heat. Add shallots; sauté 3 minutes. Stir in corn, lima beans, broth and fresh tarragon. Cook uncovered until lima beans are tender and most of broth evaporates, stirring often, about 14 minutes. *(Can be made 2 hours ahead. Let stand at room temperature.)* Add bacon and tomatoes. Cook until heated through, about 2 minutes. Season with salt and pepper.

12 SERVINGS

Red Chili Onion Rings

2 dried ancho or pasilla chilies*

2 dried guajillo or pasilla chilies*

2 large onions, cut into $1/4$-inch-thick slices, separated into rings

3 cups whole milk

1 cup all purpose flour

2 tablespoons ground cumin

2 tablespoons paprika

1 tablespoon salt

Canola oil (for deep-frying)

Two types of dried chilies spice up the coating for these crispy onion rings.

Preheat oven to 350°F. Using small sharp knife, cut stems off chilies and discard. Cut chilies open along 1 long side. Discard seeds. Place chilies on baking sheet. Roast chilies until firm and fragrant, about 5 minutes. Cool. Break chilies into small pieces. Working in batches, finely grind chilies in spice grinder or blender. *(Can be made 2 weeks ahead. Store airtight at room temperature.)*

Place onions in bowl. Pour milk over; let stand 30 minutes, tossing occasionally. Whisk flour, 2 tablespoons ground chilies, cumin, paprika and salt in large bowl to blend.

Pour enough oil into large pot to reach depth of 3 inches. Heat to 350°F. Working with a few onion rings at a time, shake off excess milk. Dip into flour mixture, coating lightly. Add onion rings to pot; deep-fry until golden, about 45 seconds. Drain on paper towels and serve.

Dried chilies are sold at Latin American markets and some supermarkets.

4 SERVINGS

Serve this crunchy *nuevo Latino-*style side dish in place of coleslaw; its updated flavors and bright colors give it extra appeal.

LATIN SPICE MIX

$1/4$ cup cumin seeds

3 tablespoons whole black peppercorns

1 tablespoon coriander seeds

2 tablespoons sugar

$1^1/2$ teaspoons sea salt

CHAYOTE SLAW

1 poblano chili*

1 red bell pepper

1 yellow bell pepper

1 tablespoon plus $1/2$ cup olive oil

4 cups matchstick-size strips pitted chayote** (from 3 medium)

$1/3$ cup Sherry wine vinegar

2 teaspoons chopped fresh cilantro

FOR LATIN SPICE MIX: Combine first 3 ingredients in heavy medium skillet. Stir over medium heat until fragrant and toasted. Cool slightly. Finely grind spices in blender. Transfer to small bowl. Mix in sugar and salt.

FOR CHAYOTE SLAW: Char chili and bell peppers over gas flame or in broiler until blackened on all sides. Enclose in plastic bag 10 minutes. Peel, seed and cut chili and peppers into matchstick-size strips.

Heat 1 tablespoon oil in heavy large skillet over medium-high heat. Add chayote and sauté just until crisp-tender, about 1 minute. Cool.

Combine Sherry wine vinegar and 2 teaspoons Latin spice mix in medium bowl (reserve remaining spice mix for use in Shrimp and Sweet Potato Cakes with Chipotle Tartar Sauce, page 12, or another use). Gradually whisk in remaining $1/2$ cup oil. Mix in fresh cilantro. Season vinaigrette to taste with salt and pepper.

Combine chayote, chili and peppers in bowl. Toss with enough vinaigrette to coat. Season to taste with salt and pepper. *(Can be prepared 1 day ahead. Cover with plastic wrap and refrigerate.)*

A fresh green chili, often called a pasilla, *available at Latin American markets and some supermarkets.*

**A squash-like, pear-shaped fruit similar in flavor to cucumber and often prepared like squash; available at Latin American markets and some supermarkets.*

6 SERVINGS

salads

Green Bean, Watercress and Walnut Salad

12	ounces green beans, trimmed, halved diagonally (about 3 cups)
$^1/_4$	cup red wine vinegar
$1^1/_2$	tablespoons Dijon mustard
1	tablespoon minced fresh parsley
$^1/_2$	cup walnut oil or olive oil
4	bunches watercress, trimmed
$1^1/_2$	cups walnuts, toasted, coarsely chopped (about 6 ounces)
$1^1/_2$	cups cherry tomatoes, halved

Cook beans in large pot of boiling salted water until crisp-tender, 4 minutes. Drain. Transfer to bowl of ice water to cool. Drain; pat dry.

Whisk vinegar, mustard and parsley in small bowl to blend. Gradually whisk in oil. Season with salt and pepper. *(Can be made 1 day ahead. Cover beans and vinaigrette separately; chill. Rewhisk vinaigrette before using.)*

Combine beans, watercress, walnuts and tomatoes in large bowl. Toss with enough vinaigrette to coat. Season to taste with salt and pepper.

10 SERVINGS

Toasting Nuts for Extra Flavor

Toasting nuts does three key things: It darkens their color to an attractive golden brown; it develops their flavor, making it richer and more pronounced; and, by evaporating some of their moisture, it gives them a crisper, crunchier texture. In addition, for some nuts with tightly clinging skins, such as hazelnuts or Brazil nuts, toasting also loosens the skins, enabling them to be rubbed off inside a folded kitchen towel while the nuts are still warm.

To toast nuts, preheat the oven to 325°F. Spread the nuts out in a single layer in a baking dish or on a rimmed baking sheet and toast until they turn a light golden in color, two to ten minutes depending on their size. Do not overcook them; nuts will continue to darken from residual heat after you remove them from the oven.

It is usually not necessary to toast nuts that will be included in thin, quickly baked goods such as cookies, which give them adequate exposure to the oven's heat. Nuts included in breads and cakes, however, may be toasted beforehand as a particular recipe requires.

Potato Salad with Olives, Beans and Red Onion

Two types of beans and two types of olives spruce up a potato salad.

2/3 cup olive oil

1/4 cup white wine vinegar

2 tablespoons minced shallots

4 anchovies, minced

2 teaspoons chopped fresh parsley

2 teaspoons chopped fresh basil

2 teaspoons chopped fresh marjoram

8 ounces green beans, trimmed

8 ounces yellow wax beans, trimmed

2 pounds Yukon Gold potatoes, unpeeled, cut into 1/2-inch cubes

1/2 cup chopped red onion

1/2 cup green olives, pitted, halved

1/2 cup Niçois olives,* pitted, halved

1/4 cup drained capers

Mix oil, vinegar, shallots and anchovies in medium bowl. Whisk in 1 teaspoon each of parsley, basil and marjoram. Season with salt and pepper.

Cook all beans in large saucepan of boiling salted water until crisp-tender, about 5 minutes. Drain. Rinse beans under cold water; pat dry.

Steam potatoes until just tender, about 12 minutes. Transfer to large bowl. Heat dressing in microwave just until warm, about 30 seconds. Pour half of warm dressing over potatoes and toss to coat. Mound warm potatoes in center of platter. Toss beans and remaining dressing in same bowl. Arrange beans around potatoes. Sprinkle with onion, all olives, capers and remaining herbs. Serve warm or at room temperature.

Available at Italian markets, specialty foods stores and some supermarkets.

10 SERVINGS

Hoppin' John Salad

6¹/₂ cups (or more) chicken stock or canned low-salt chicken broth
2 cups dried black-eyed peas
2 bay leaves
3 teaspoons minced fresh thyme
¹/₈ teaspoon plus ¹/₄ teaspoon cayenne pepper

1¹/₄ cups water
²/₃ cup long-grain white rice
¹/₄ teaspoon salt

¹/₂ cup corn oil or olive oil
3 tablespoons apple cider vinegar
1 cup chopped red and/or yellow bell pepper
¹/₂ cup chopped red onion
   Red lettuce leaves

Combine 6¹/₂ cups stock, black-eyed peas, bay leaves, 2 teaspoons thyme and ¹/₈ teaspoon cayenne pepper in heavy large saucepan. Bring to boil. Reduce heat; simmer uncovered until black-eyed peas are tender, adding more stock if necessary to keep peas submerged and stirring occasionally, about 1¹/₄ hours. Drain well; discard broth and bay leaves. Transfer black-eyed peas to large bowl.

Bring 1¹/₄ cups water to boil in medium saucepan. Add rice and salt. Bring to boil. Reduce heat to low; cover and cook until rice is tender and water is absorbed, 20 minutes. Transfer to bowl with black-eyed peas.

Whisk oil, vinegar, 1 teaspoon thyme and ¹/₄ teaspoon cayenne in small bowl. Add dressing to black-eyed pea mixture; toss. Stir in bell pepper and red onion. Season with salt and pepper. Chill at least 45 minutes and up to 6 hours. Arrange lettuce on plates. Spoon salad into lettuce.

4 SERVINGS

Soul Food Is Back

As evidenced by the popularity of barbecue joints and the appearance of biscuits, grits and greens on the menus of upscale restaurants, southern-style cooking is making a comeback—nationwide. Here are some of the signature ingredients in this trend; all may be found in well-stocked supermarkets.

- Bourbon: The smooth, slightly smoky form of whiskey is made from fermented grain. From Kentucky, it's a favorite in cocktails, and it appears as a flavoring in sweet and savory dishes.
- Catfish: The sweet, tender meat of this freshwater fish is winning diners over; today's farm-raised catfish lack the muddy aftertaste of the wild ones.
- Greens: Abounding in calcium, these robust, pleasantly bitter leaves include collard greens, kale, mustard greens and Swiss chard.
- Grits: This hominy mush is a southern staple. See "All in the Polenta Family," page 97.
- Okra: Best when bite-size, these gray-green pods are enjoyed sautéed, simmered, deep-fried or pickled, and are used in stews and gumbos.
- Pecans: The sweet, rich taste of pecans is enjoyed in such classic desserts as pecan pie as well as in candies. They appear in savory dishes, or chopped as coatings for fried poultry or seafood.

Green Bean, Yellow Bean and Cherry Tomato Salad

Fourth of July Picnic for Four

Citrus-marinated Olives
(page 21)

Roasted Chicken, Zucchini and Ricotta Sandwiches on Foccaccia
(page 81)

Green Bean, Yellow Bean and Cherry Tomato Salad
(at left; pictured opposite)

Potato Salad

White Wine or Lemonade

Watermelon

³/₄ pound green beans, trimmed

³/₄ pound yellow wax beans, trimmed

3 cups cherry tomatoes (about 14 ounces), halved

1 medium-size red onion, thinly sliced

¹/₂ cup thinly sliced fresh basil

5 tablespoons extra-virgin olive oil

3 tablespoons red wine vinegar

¹/₄ teaspoon sugar

Cook all beans in large pot of boiling salted water until crisp-tender, 5 minutes. Drain; rinse with cold water and drain well.

Combine beans, tomatoes, onion and basil in serving bowl. Whisk olive oil, vinegar and sugar in small bowl to blend. Season dressing to taste with salt and pepper. Add dressing to vegetables; toss to coat. Cover and refrigerate at least 1 hour and up to 4 hours, tossing occasionally. Serve salad cold or at room temperature.

6 SERVINGS

Radicchio, Grapefruit and Spinach Salad

5 tablespoons red wine vinegar

1 teaspoon fennel seeds, crushed

¹/₂ cup olive oil

2 white grapefruits

1 10-ounce head radicchio, torn into bite-size pieces

8 ounces baby spinach leaves

¹/₂ cup Kalamata olives or other brine-cured black olives, pitted

Combine vinegar and fennel seeds in medium bowl. Gradually whisk in oil. Season dressing with salt and pepper. Cut all peel and white pith from grapefruits. Cut grapefruits between membranes to release segments. Stir segments into dressing. Let stand at least 15 minutes and up to 1 hour.

Toss radicchio, spinach and olives in bowl. Add grapefruit segments and dressing; toss to coat. Season to taste with salt and pepper.

6 SERVINGS

Fire-roasted Tomato and Bread Salad with Spicy Vinaigrette

A brief stint on the grill gives the tomatoes smoky flavor. They're tossed with chunks of bread and left to stand for 30 minutes while the bread absorbs the tomato juices. A spicy vinaigrette ties it all together.

8 tablespoons olive oil
4 large tomatoes (about 2¹/₄ pounds), halved horizontally
8 ³/₄-inch-thick crusty country-style bread slices (each about 5x3 inches)

¹/₃ cup red wine vinegar
1 teaspoon minced canned chipotle chili*
1 garlic clove, minced

¹/₂ red onion, chopped
¹/₂ cup chopped fresh cilantro

Preheat barbecue (medium-high heat). Brush 2 tablespoons oil over cut sides of tomatoes. Grill, cut side down, just until grill marks show but tomatoes are still slightly firm, 2 minutes. Turn over; grill 2 minutes longer. Transfer to baking sheet. Cool slightly. Brush 2 tablespoons oil over both sides of bread. Grill until golden, 2 minutes per side. Transfer to sheet with tomatoes.

Whisk vinegar, chili and garlic in medium bowl to blend. Gradually whisk in remaining 4 tablespoons oil. Season with salt and pepper.

Cut grilled tomatoes into ³/₄-inch pieces. Cut bread into ¹/₂-inch pieces. Combine tomatoes, bread and onion in large bowl. Toss to blend. Let stand until bread absorbs most of tomato juices, about 30 minutes. Add vinaigrette and cilantro and toss to blend. Season salad with salt and pepper.

*Chipotle *chilies canned in a spicy tomato sauce, sometimes called* adobo, *are available at Latin American markets and some supermarkets.*

6 SERVINGS

Spinach and Roasted Beet Salad with Ginger Vinaigrette

4 medium beets, trimmed

3 tablespoons rice vinegar
2 tablespoons vegetable oil
2 teaspoons reduced-sodium soy sauce
2 teaspoons minced peeled fresh ginger
¹/₂ medium red onion, thinly sliced

8 cups fresh spinach leaves (about 8 ounces), trimmed

Preheat oven to 450°F. Wrap beets in foil. Roast beets until tender when pierced with skewer, about 1 hour 15 minutes. Cool beets slightly. Peel beets; cut into wedges. Place in medium bowl.

Whisk vinegar, oil, soy sauce and ginger in small bowl to blend well. Season vinaigrette to taste with salt and pepper. Add red onion and half of vinaigrette to beets and toss to blend.

Place spinach in large bowl. Drizzle remaining vinaigrette over; toss to coat. Arrange beet mixture atop spinach and serve.

4 SERVINGS

Fennel and Apple Salad with Cider Vinaigrette

$^1/_2$ cup unfiltered apple cider or apple juice
3 tablespoons extra-virgin olive oil
2 tablespoons apple cider vinegar
1 teaspoon honey
1 large Granny Smith apple, quartered, cored, thinly sliced
1 medium-size fresh fennel bulb, trimmed, thinly sliced
2 cups arugula (about 3 ounces)
$^1/_2$ cup pecans (about 2 ounces), toasted

The quick-to-make cider vinaigrette brings out the apple flavor in this simple salad.

Whisk first 4 ingredients in medium bowl to blend; season dressing with salt and pepper. Combine apple, fennel and arugula in large bowl. Toss with enough dressing to coat. Mound salad on 4 plates; sprinkle with pecans.

4 SERVINGS

Chopsticks 1-2-3

Using chopsticks may feel awkward at first, but all it takes is a little practice. Remember—once the chopsticks are in place, the lower one will remain stationary and the upper one will do the moving. Follow these three easy steps.

Step 1: Cradle the stationary chopstick in the soft part of your hand between your thumb and index finger. Close your thumb to hold the chopstick in place. Curve your ring finger inward so that it points toward you, and rest the lower end of the chopstick on the first joint of that finger. Curve your middle finger in the same direction as your ring finger, resting your fingertip on the outside of the chopstick.

Step 2: Adjust the movable chopstick so that it rests on the first joint of the middle finger; the upper portion will naturally fall on the large joint of your index finger. The chopsticks should be parallel, with the tips lined up about an inch apart.

Step 3: Now that your chopsticks are positioned correctly, you should be able to bring the tip of the movable one to meet the tip of the stationary one in a pincerlike motion by flexing your index finger and thumb.

Japanese-Style Quick-pickled Slaw

$^1/_2$ cup rice vinegar
2 tablespoons oriental sesame oil
2 tablespoons soy sauce
1 tablespoon golden brown sugar
1 tablespoon minced peeled fresh ginger
1 tablespoon Thai fish sauce (nam pla)*
1 medium cucumber, peeled, seeded, cut into matchstick-size strips
1 large carrot, peeled, cut into matchstick-size strips
1 red bell pepper, cut into matchstick-size strips
4 cups thinly sliced Napa cabbage

Whisk first 6 ingredients in medium saucepan. Bring to boil; pour into large bowl. Add cucumber, carrot and red bell pepper. Cool. Add cabbage to vegetable mixture; toss to blend. Season to taste with salt.

Available at Asian markets and in the Asian foods section of some supermarkets.

6 SERVINGS

Mixed Greens with Roasted Asparagus and Apple

24 thin asparagus spears, ends trimmed
1 tablespoon plus $^1/_3$ cup olive oil

$^1/_4$ cup rice vinegar
2 tablespoons honey
1 garlic clove, minced
2 5-ounce packages mixed baby greens
1 Golden Delicious apple, quartered, cored, diced
4 ounces Gruyère cheese, cut into thin ribbons with vegetable peeler

Preheat oven to 400°F. Arrange asparagus in single layer on baking sheet. Drizzle with 1 tablespoon oil; sprinkle with salt and pepper. Toss to coat. Roast asparagus 30 minutes, turning once. Cool 5 minutes.

Meanwhile, whisk remaining $^1/_3$ cup oil, vinegar, honey and garlic in small bowl to blend. Place greens in large bowl. Add vinaigrette to greens; toss to coat. Mound salad on each of 8 plates. Top with apple and cheese, dividing equally. Arrange asparagus on top.

8 SERVINGS

The Flavors of Bon Appétit 2001

Farro Salad with Peas, Favas, Arugula and Tomatoes

6 cups water
2 cups farro or wheat berries*
5 tablespoons olive oil
2¹/₂ tablespoons red wine vinegar

1 cup shelled fresh fava beans** or frozen baby lima beans
1 cup shelled fresh peas or frozen peas

2 cups fresh arugula leaves, halved
3 plum tomatoes, seeded, finely chopped
Additional arugula leaves

Combine 6 cups water and farro in medium saucepan. Bring to boil. Reduce heat to medium. Cover partially and simmer until farro is tender, about 20 minutes (about 45 minutes for wheat berries). Drain well. Whisk oil and vinegar in large bowl to blend. Season to taste with salt. Add farro and toss to coat. Cool.

Meanwhile, cook favas in pot of boiling salted water 3 minutes. Add peas and cook until just tender, about 1 minute longer. Drain. Cool in bowl of ice water. Drain. Add favas and peas to farro. *(Can be prepared 4 hours ahead. Cover and refrigerate.)*

Add arugula and tomatoes to farro mixture. Toss to combine. Season salad generously with salt. Spoon onto platter. Garnish with additional arugula and serve.

Farro is sold at some Italian markets. Wheat berries are sold at natural foods stores and some supermarkets.
**Available at Middle Eastern markets and some supermarkets.*

8 SERVINGS

Bread doughs can have different consistencies depending on the climate; this one should be soft but not too sticky. Add more flour if it feels too wet.

1 cup lukewarm water (90°F to 100°F)

2 ¹/₄-ounce packages dry yeast or two 0.6-ounce packages fresh yeast, crumbled

2¹/₂ cups (about) all purpose flour

4 tablespoons extra-virgin olive oil

1 tablespoon coarse sea salt

Pour 1 cup lukewarm water into small bowl; sprinkle with yeast. Let stand until yeast dissolves, about 10 minutes.

Place 2 cups flour in large bowl. Make well in center of flour. Pour yeast mixture into well. Using fork, stir until dough comes together. Knead dough in bowl, adding enough flour ¹/₄ cup at a time to form slightly sticky dough. Transfer to floured work surface. Knead until dough is smooth and elastic, about 10 minutes. Coat bowl with 1 tablespoon olive oil. Add dough; turn to coat. Cover bowl with plastic wrap. Let stand in warm draft-free area until doubled in volume, about 1 hour 15 minutes.

Brush 11-inch-diameter tart pan with removable bottom or baking sheet with 1 tablespoon olive oil. Punch down dough. Turn dough out onto floured work surface and shape into 11-inch round. Transfer dough to prepared tart pan or baking sheet. Cover dough loosely with plastic wrap. Let rise until dough is almost doubled in volume, about 30 minutes.

Preheat oven to 400°F. Press fingertips into dough, creating indentations. Brush with remaining 2 tablespoons olive oil. Sprinkle with sea salt. Bake bread until golden, about 28 minutes. Cool bread in pan on rack 10 minutes. Remove bread from pan and cool completely.

MAKES 1 ROUND LOAF

breads

Cheddar Cheese Biscuits

  2 cups unbleached all purpose flour
  1 tablespoon baking powder
  1 tablespoon sugar
  1 teaspoon salt
$^1/_2$ cup (1 stick) chilled unsalted butter, cut into pieces
  1 cup (packed) coarsely grated extra-sharp cheddar cheese (about 4 ounces)
$^2/_3$ cup (or more) cold whole milk

Preheat oven to 450°F. Whisk first 4 ingredients in medium bowl to blend. Rub in butter with fingertips until pea-size pieces form. Add cheese and rub with fingertips. Add $^2/_3$ cup milk, tossing mixture with fork until dough begins to come together and adding more milk by tablespoonfuls if dry (do not overmix). Gather dough together.

Turn dough out onto floured surface. Pat into $^1/_2$-inch-thick round. Cut into 2-inch rounds. Gather scraps, reshape and cut out additional rounds. Transfer biscuits to ungreased baking sheet, spacing 1 inch apart. Bake until golden brown, about 15 minutes. Serve warm or at room temperature.

MAKES ABOUT 17

These tender, flaky biscuits are terrific with breakfast, lunch or dinner. They come together quickly and bake in just 15 minutes.

Cinnamon Popovers

    Nonstick vegetable oil spray
  1 cup whole milk
  2 large eggs
  1 teaspoon vanilla extract
$^1/_2$ teaspoon ground cinnamon
$^1/_4$ teaspoon salt
  1 cup all purpose flour
    Powdered sugar

Preheat oven to 450°F. Spray nine $^1/_3$-cup muffin cups with nonstick spray. Whisk milk, eggs, vanilla, cinnamon and salt in medium bowl to blend. Add flour; whisk until smooth. Divide batter among muffin cups.

Bake 15 minutes. Reduce oven temperature to 350°F. Continue to bake popovers until brown and crisp, about 20 minutes. Turn out of pan, loosening with small sharp knife. Sift sugar over and serve.

MAKES 9

Country Hearth Bread

It's best to begin this bread the day before you plan to serve it because the starter needs to sit for at least four hours (and up to one day), and the bread dough has to rise twice before it is baked.

STARTER

2/3 cup whole milk, room temperature
2/3 cup warm water (105°F to 115°F)
1 teaspoon dry yeast
1 teaspoon honey
1³/4 cups unbleached all purpose flour

DOUGH

1 teaspoon dry yeast
1¹/2 cups water, room temperature
5¹/2 cups (about) unbleached all purpose flour
¹/4 cup olive oil
4 teaspoons salt

FOR STARTER: Combine milk and ²/3 cup warm water in large bowl. Sprinkle yeast over; stir to blend. Let stand until dissolved, about 10 minutes. Add honey and then flour, ¹/2 cup at a time, whisking until smooth (mixture will be thick and sticky). Cover loosely with plastic wrap; let stand 4 hours (mixture will be thick and bubbly). *(Can be prepared 1 day ahead. Refrigerate overnight. Bring to room temperature before using.)*

FOR DOUGH: Using electric mixer with paddle attachment, beat yeast, then 1¹/2 cups water, 1 cup flour, oil and salt into starter. Continue beating on medium-low speed 2 minutes. Beat in enough flour, ¹/2 cup at a time, to form smooth yet sticky dough (dough will not pull away from sides of bowl). Scrape dough out onto floured work surface. Knead until smooth and elastic, adding more flour by tablespoonfuls if necessary to prevent sticking, about 5 minutes. Let dough rest uncovered 5 minutes. Form into ball. Place in large ungreased bowl. Cover with plastic. Let rise in warm draft-free area until doubled, about 1 hour 15 minutes.

Flour baking sheet. Punch down dough. Turn out onto floured work surface. Divide in half. Shape each piece into 6-inch round. Place on baking sheet. Let rise uncovered in warm draft-free area until doubled, 1 hour.

Position rack in center of oven and preheat to 400°F. Using sharp knife, cut ¹/2-inch-deep, 3-inch-long diagonal slashes, forming X in top of each loaf. Dust tops lightly with flour. Bake until loaves are deep golden and sound hollow when tapped on bottom, about 35 minutes. Cool on rack. *(Can be prepared ahead of time. Wrap in foil and store at room temperature 1 day or freeze up to 2 weeks.)*

MAKES 2 LOAVES

Pumpkin-Walnut Bread

2 cups all purpose flour

1 teaspoon baking soda

1 teaspoon baking powder

1 teaspoon salt

$^1/_2$ teaspoon ground cinnamon

$^1/_2$ teaspoon ground cloves

$^1/_2$ teaspoon ground ginger

$^1/_2$ cup (1 stick) unsalted butter, room temperature

$^3/_4$ cup plus 1 tablespoon sugar

2 large eggs, room temperature

1 cup canned pure pumpkin

$1^1/_2$ teaspoons grated lemon peel

1 teaspoon vanilla extract

$^1/_2$ cup sour cream

$^1/_2$ cup whole milk

$1^1/_2$ cups chopped walnuts

Serve slices of this nut-studded quick bread with purchased cranberry preserves.

Position rack in center of oven; preheat to 325°F. Butter 9x5x3-inch metal loaf pan. Sift first 7 ingredients into medium bowl. Using electric mixer, beat butter in large bowl until light. Gradually beat in $^3/_4$ cup sugar. Beat in eggs 1 at a time. Beat in pumpkin, lemon peel and vanilla. Whisk sour cream and milk in small bowl. Beat flour and sour cream mixtures alternately into batter in 2 additions each. Fold in nuts. Transfer batter to pan; smooth top. Sprinkle with 1 tablespoon sugar.

Bake bread until tester inserted into center comes out clean, about 1 hour 10 minutes. Cool in pan 10 minutes. Turn out onto rack; cool. *(Can be made 2 days ahead. Wrap in foil; store at room temperature.)*

MAKES 1 LOAF

Orange and Cream Scones

4 cups all purpose flour

$1/2$ cup sugar

2 tablespoons grated orange peel

4 teaspoons baking powder

1 teaspoon salt

$1^1/_4$ cups ($2^1/_2$ sticks) chilled unsalted butter, cut into $^1/_2$-inch cubes

2 large eggs, lightly beaten

1 cup chilled half and half

Additional sugar

Preheat oven to 375°F. Line 2 large baking sheets with parchment paper. Whisk first 5 ingredients in large bowl to blend. Rub in butter with fingertips until flour mixture resembles coarse crumbs.

Beat eggs and half and half in medium bowl to blend. Stir into flour mixture, tossing until dough comes together (dough will be moist). Turn out onto floured work surface. Knead gently, about 6 turns. Divide dough in half; pat each half into 7-inch round. Cut each round into 6 wedges; transfer to baking sheets, spacing wedges apart. Sprinkle with additional sugar.

Bake scones until golden on bottom and beginning to color on top, 25 minutes. Serve warm or let stand up to 3 hours.

MAKES 12

Molasses and Oat Soda Bread

Serve wedges of this hearty, raisin-flecked bread with purchased apple butter.

Yellow cornmeal

$1^1/_4$ cups buttermilk

$^1/_4$ cup mild-flavored (light) molasses

2 tablespoons vegetable oil

$1^1/_2$ cups old-fashioned oats

3 cups unbleached all purpose flour

$^1/_2$ cup whole wheat flour

1 tablespoon sugar

$1^1/_2$ teaspoons salt

1 teaspoon baking soda

1 teaspoon baking powder

1 cup raisins

Preheat oven to 400°F. Lightly oil large baking sheet; sprinkle with cornmeal. Whisk buttermilk, molasses and oil in medium bowl. Stir in oats; set aside. Mix next 6 ingredients in large bowl. Make well in center. Add buttermilk mixture and raisins. Stir until dough comes together (it will be moist). Let stand 5 minutes.

Lightly flour work surface. Scoop half of dough onto surface; knead gently just until no longer sticky, about 30 seconds. Shape dough into 4 1/2-inch-diameter ball. Repeat with remaining dough. Place loaves on baking sheet, spacing evenly. Using sharp serrated knife, make 2 parallel slashes atop each loaf, about 3/4 inch deep.

Bake loaves 20 minutes. Reduce heat to 375°F. Bake until loaves are dark and crusty and sound hollow when tapped on bottom, about 25 minutes. Transfer to rack; cool. *(Can be made 8 hours ahead.)*

MAKES 2 LOAVES

Chocolate Crunch Layer Cake with Milk Chocolate Frosting
(page 174)

Desserts

pies & tarts
fruit desserts
cakes
mousses & puddings
frozen desserts
cookies

Apple and Caraway Tartlets with Cider-Caramel Sauce

Try the Cider-Caramel Sauce over vanilla, cinnamon or caramel ice cream for a new kind of sundae. Sprinkle with toasted walnuts and top with whipped cream, if desired.

CRUST

1¹/₂ cups all purpose flour

3 tablespoons sugar

1 teaspoon caraway seeds

¹/₂ teaspoon salt

¹/₂ cup (1 stick) chilled unsalted butter, cut into ¹/₂-inch cubes

5 teaspoons (or more) ice water

FILLING

Cider-Caramel Sauce (see recipe opposite)

2¹/₂ pounds medium Granny Smith apples (about 7), peeled, halved, cored, each half cut into 4 wedges

¹/₂ teaspoon ground cinnamon

Vanilla ice cream
Clusters of red grapes (optional)
Fresh mint (optional)

FOR CRUST: Blend flour, sugar, caraway seeds and salt in processor. Add butter and process using on/off turns until butter is cut into pea-size pieces. Add 5 teaspoons ice water. Blend until moist clumps form, adding more ice water by teaspoonfuls if dough is dry. Gather dough into ball; flatten into disk. Cut into 6 equal pieces. Press each piece of dough into 4¹/2-inch-diameter tartlet pan with ³/4-inch-high sides and removable bottom. *(Can be made 1 day ahead. Cover each crust and refrigerate.)*

FOR FILLING: Place ³/4 cup Cider-Caramel Sauce in heavy large skillet. Add apples and cinnamon. Cook over high heat until apples are crisp-tender, about 8 minutes. Cool filling completely.

Place rack in bottom third of oven; preheat to 375°F. Divide filling among crusts, overlapping apples if desired. Place tartlets on oven rack; bake until apples are tender and crust is brown at edges, about 40 minutes. Transfer to rack; cool 30 minutes. Push up pan bottoms, releasing tartlets. *(Can be made 8 hours ahead. Let stand at room temperature.)*

Rewarm remaining sauce in saucepan. Place tartlets on plates. Top with ice cream and warm sauce. Garnish with grapes and mint, if desired.

MAKES 6

pies & tarts

Cider-Caramel Sauce

    4 cups apple cider
    1 vanilla bean, split lengthwise
  $^1/_2$ cup (packed) dark brown sugar
  $^1/_4$ cup ($^1/_2$ stick) unsalted butter

Place cider in heavy large skillet. Scrape in seeds from vanilla bean; add bean. Boil cider mixture until reduced to 2 cups, about 15 minutes. Add sugar and butter. Cook until sauce thickens slightly and is reduced to $1^1/2$ cups, stirring occasionally, about 6 minutes longer. *(Can be prepared 3 days ahead. Transfer to small bowl. Cover and refrigerate. Remove vanilla bean before using.)*

MAKES $1^1/_2$ CUPS

Blueberry Pie with Lattice Crust

A scalloped pastry cutter makes the lattice strips look as if they've been cut out with pinking shears. You can weave the strips or not when you're making the lattice top—it works either way.

CRUST

2¹/₂ cups all purpose flour

1¹/₂ tablespoons sugar

1¹/₄ teaspoons salt

²/₃ cup solid vegetable shortening, frozen, then cut into ¹/₂-inch cubes

¹/₂ cup (1 stick) chilled unsalted butter, cut into ¹/₂-inch cubes

6 tablespoons (or more) ice water

2 teaspoons apple cider vinegar

FILLING

4 ¹/₂-pint baskets blueberries

³/₄ cup sugar

¹/₄ cup all purpose flour

2 tablespoons fresh lemon juice

1 teaspoon grated lemon peel

1 teaspoon vanilla extract

Whipping cream (for glaze)

FOR CRUST: Blend flour, sugar and salt in processor. Add shortening and butter and cut in, using on/off turns, until mixture resembles coarse meal. Transfer to bowl. Mix 6 tablespoons ice water and vinegar in small bowl; pour over flour mixture. Stir with fork until moist clumps form, adding more ice water by teaspoonfuls if dry. Gather dough into 2 balls; flatten each into disk. Wrap each in plastic and chill 30 minutes.

FOR FILLING: Position rack in bottom third of oven; preheat to 400°F. Combine first 6 ingredients in bowl. Crush a few blueberries with back of rubber spatula; toss to blend. Let stand about 15 minutes.

Roll out 1 pie crust on floured surface to 12¹/₂-inch round. Transfer to 9-inch-diameter pie dish. Trim dough overhang to ³/₄ inch. Spoon filling into crust. Roll out second pie crust to 12-inch round. Using scalloped pastry cutter, cut dough into generous ¹/₂-inch-wide strips. Arrange half of dough strips across top of filling. Form lattice by arranging more dough strips at right angle to first strips, weaving if desired. Trim strips even with overhang. Tuck ends of dough strips and overhang under; press to seal. Crimp edges decoratively; brush lightly with cream.

Place pie on baking sheet. Bake 40 minutes. Cover crust edges with foil to prevent overbrowning. Continue to bake until filling bubbles thickly in center, about 50 minutes longer. Cool pie on rack 2 hours.

8 SERVINGS

Plum Tart with Marzipan Topping

CRUST

1 cup all purpose flour

$^3/_4$ cup sliced almonds

$^1/_4$ cup sugar

$^1/_8$ teaspoon salt

$^1/_2$ cup (1 stick) chilled unsalted butter, cut into $^1/_2$-inch cubes

2 tablespoons chilled whipping cream

1 large egg yolk

TOPPING

$^3/_4$ cup all purpose flour

$^1/_2$ cup (packed) almond paste (about 5 ounces)

$^1/_2$ cup (packed) golden brown sugar

6 tablespoons ($^3/_4$ stick) chilled unsalted butter, cut into $^1/_2$-inch cubes

$^1/_4$ cup sliced almonds

FILLING

$2^1/_4$ pounds plums (about 12), halved, pitted, thinly sliced

$^1/_2$ cup sugar

2 tablespoons plus 2 teaspoons cornstarch

Make this recipe in the summer months, when plums are in season. The nutty marzipan topping is a delicious contrast to the sweet-tart filling.

FOR CRUST: Blend first 4 ingredients in processor until nuts are finely ground. Add butter; process until mixture resembles coarse meal. Add cream and yolk. Using on/off turns, blend until dough comes together. Press over bottom and up sides of 11-inch-diameter tart pan with removable bottom. Pierce all over with fork. Chill at least 2 hours and up to 1 day.

Preheat oven to 400°F. Bake crust until golden, pressing with back of fork every 5 minutes if crust bubbles, about 25 minutes. Transfer crust to rack; cool. Reduce oven temperature to 375°F.

FOR TOPPING: Blend flour, almond paste and sugar in processor until almond paste is finely ground. Add butter and process using on/off turns until coarse crumbs form. Transfer to bowl; mix in almonds.

FOR FILLING: Combine all ingredients in medium bowl; toss to blend well.

Sprinkle $^3/_4$ cup marzipan topping over cooled crust. Top with plums. Sprinkle plums with remaining topping.

Bake tart until filling bubbles thickly and top is golden, about 40 minutes. Cool 10 minutes. Push up pan bottom to release tart. Cool. *(Can be made 8 hours ahead. Let stand at room temperature.)*

10 TO 12 SERVINGS

Lemon-Pistachio Tart

CRUST

1¹/₂ cups all purpose flour

¹/₄ teaspoon salt

¹/₂ cup (1 stick) chilled unsalted butter, cut into ¹/₂-inch cubes

1 large egg yolk

3 tablespoons (or more) ice water

FILLING

1 cup (2 sticks) unsalted butter

1 cup plus 2 tablespoons sugar

¹/₃ cup fresh lemon juice

3 large eggs

3 large egg yolks

1 tablespoon grated lemon peel

1¹/₂ teaspoons vanilla extract

4 teaspoons water

¹/₂ cup unsalted shelled pistachios

The tart and the candied pistachios can both be prepared one day ahead. Cover and refrigerate the tart; store the pistachios airtight at room temperature. Before serving, let the tart stand at room temperature 20 minutes, then sprinkle the edge with the pistachios.

FOR CRUST: Combine flour and salt in processor. Cut in butter using on/off turns until mixture resembles coarse meal. Add yolk and 3 tablespoons ice water. Process until moist clumps form, adding more water by teaspoonfuls if dry. Gather into ball; flatten into disk. Wrap in plastic; chill 30 minutes. *(Can be made 1 day ahead. Keep chilled.)*

Preheat oven to 375°F. Roll out dough on lightly floured surface to 12-inch round. Transfer dough to 9-inch-diameter tart pan with removable bottom. Fold in overhang and press, forming high-standing rim. Pierce all over with fork. Cover and freeze 20 minutes.

Bake crust until deep golden, about 40 minutes. Transfer to rack; cool.

FOR FILLING: Melt butter in heavy medium saucepan over medium heat. Whisk in 1 cup sugar and next 5 ingredients. Cook until mixture thickens, whisking constantly, about 10 minutes. Reduce heat to low and whisk 2 minutes longer. Pour hot filling into baked crust. Chill uncovered until filling is set, at least 2 hours and up to 1 day.

Line baking sheet with foil. Stir 2 tablespoons sugar and 4 teaspoons water in small saucepan over low heat until sugar dissolves. Increase heat; boil without stirring until pale golden, 6 minutes. Add pistachios; stir to coat. Spread in single layer on sheet. Cool. Coarsely chop.

Sprinkle pistachios in 2-inch border around edge of tart and serve.

6 SERVINGS

Chocolate-Mint Brownie Tart

1 refrigerated pie crust (half of 15-ounce package), chilled

5 tablespoons unsalted butter

1 19- to 20-ounce box double chocolate brownie mix

8 tablespoons plus 4 teaspoons water

1 large egg

$^1/_2$ teaspoon peppermint extract

$^3/_4$ cup semisweet chocolate chips

$^3/_4$ cup white baking chips

Fresh mint sprigs

A refrigerated pie crust and a purchased brownie mix take most of the work out of this impressive-looking tart. Serve with vanilla or mint chocolate chip ice cream.

Preheat oven to 350°F. Unfold crust into 9-inch-diameter tart pan with removable bottom. Fold in overhang and press firmly to sides. Using fingertips, press sides up to form raised edge $^1/_8$ inch above pan sides. Pierce crust all over with fork. Freeze 5 minutes. Bake crust until golden, about 22 minutes. Cool. Maintain oven temperature.

Melt butter in heavy small saucepan over low heat; pour into large bowl. Add brownie mix, 5 tablespoons plus 1 teaspoon water, egg and peppermint extract; whisk to blend well. Stir in packet of chocolate chips, if included in brownie mix.

Spoon batter into crust. Bake until tester inserted into center comes out with some moist crumbs still attached, about 45 minutes. Let stand on rack while preparing chocolate toppings.

Whisk $^3/_4$ cup semisweet chips and 2 tablespoons plus 2 teaspoons water in heavy small saucepan over low heat until melted and smooth. Remove from heat. Combine white baking chips with 1 tablespoon plus 1 teaspoon water in another heavy small saucepan. Whisk over low heat until melted and smooth. Remove from heat.

Spoon melted semisweet chocolate by tablespoonfuls onto warm brownie in 7 or 8 pools, spacing evenly. Spoon melted white chips into remaining spaces to cover brownie. Using tip of knife, swirl chocolates. Let cool at room temperature in pan on rack until top is set, about 2 hours. *(Can be made 1 day ahead. Cover; let stand at room temperature.)* Remove tart pan sides. Garnish with mint and serve.

10 SERVINGS

Cherry Crumble Pie

If cherries are in season, use the fresh ones; if not, frozen cherries will work fine here. The "crumble" topping is a delicious mixture of old-fashioned oats, brown sugar, almonds and cinnamon.

CRUST

$1^1/_2$ cups all purpose flour

1 tablespoon sugar

$^1/_4$ teaspoon salt

6 tablespoons chilled unsalted butter, cut into $^1/_2$-inch cubes

2 tablespoons chilled vegetable shortening, cut into $^1/_2$-inch cubes

2 tablespoons (or more) ice water

1 large egg yolk

FILLING

  6 cups fresh cherries, pitted, or 2 pounds frozen pitted sweet cherries,
     thawed, juices reserved
  1 cup sugar
2$^{1}/_{2}$ tablespoons quick-cooking tapioca
  1 tablespoon kirsch (clear cherry brandy) or brandy
     Pinch of salt

TOPPING

  1 cup plus 2 tablespoons old-fashioned oats
$^{3}/_{4}$ cup all purpose flour
$^{3}/_{4}$ cup (packed) golden brown sugar
$^{1}/_{2}$ cup sliced almonds
$^{3}/_{4}$ teaspoon ground cinnamon
$^{1}/_{4}$ teaspoon salt
$^{1}/_{2}$ cup (1 stick) chilled unsalted butter, cut into $^{1}/_{2}$-inch cubes

FOR CRUST: Blend flour, sugar and salt in processor 5 seconds. Add butter and shortening and process using on/off turns until mixture resembles coarse meal. Beat 2 tablespoons ice water and yolk in bowl to blend. Add to dough. Using on/off turns, blend until moist clumps form, adding more ice water by teaspoonfuls if dough is dry. Gather dough into ball; flatten into disk. Wrap in plastic; chill at least 30 minutes and up to 1 day.

FOR FILLING: Mix cherries and juices, sugar, tapioca, kirsch and salt in bowl. Let stand until tapioca looks translucent, stirring occasionally, 1 hour.

FOR TOPPING: Blend oats, flour, sugar, almonds, cinnamon and salt in large bowl. Add butter. Rub in with fingertips, pressing mixture together until moist clumps form; chill until ready to use.

Preheat oven to 425°F. Roll out dough on lightly floured surface to 13- to 14-inch round. Transfer to 9-inch-diameter deep-dish glass pie dish. Trim overhang to $^{3}/_{4}$ inch; fold under. Crimp edge decoratively. Spoon filling into dough-lined dish. Sprinkle with topping.

Bake pie 30 minutes. Reduce temperature to 400°F. Continue to bake until filling bubbles thickly and topping is brown and crisp, covering edges with foil if browning too quickly, about 25 minutes longer. Cool at least 30 minutes. Serve warm or at room temperature.

6 TO 8 SERVINGS

Perfecting Pie Crusts

The old phrase *easy as pie* can be true for you—just keep these tips in mind when making pie crust.

- Patch It Up: When lining a pie pan with dough, pinch together any tears, or seal with pastry trimmings.
- Line It Loosely: To prevent shrinkage during baking, don't stretch the dough when lining the pan. Drape the dough in loosely, then gently press it into the pan's contours.
- Trim and Crimp: For a perfect rim that won't shrink, trim the dough evenly and tuck it under itself along the pan's rim. Crimp the dough between your fingers or with fork tines or a pastry crimper.
- Blind-Bake When Necessary: Pierce the dough a few times with a fork (to keep bubbles from forming) and line the dough with foil. The foil is held in place with dried beans, rice or specially designed ceramic or aluminum pie weights. After the crust has baked for 10 to 15 minutes, the weights and lining are removed, and the crust bakes until just brown or until cooked through, depending on the recipe.
- Shield the Crust Edges: If a pie is not fully baked but its crust edges appear to be browning too quickly, shield them from overbaking by gently covering with strips of aluminum foil, placed shiny side out to reflect the oven's heat.

Cherries Simmered in Red Wine

Choose a Chianti to use in this recipe for a truly authentic rendition of this classic Italian dessert.

4 cups dry red wine

1¹/₂ cups sugar

2 pounds red or golden cherries, stemmed, pitted

¹/₂ teaspoon grated orange peel

¹/₈ teaspoon almond extract

¹/₈ teaspoon ground nutmeg

Stir wine and sugar in heavy large saucepan over medium heat until sugar dissolves. Add cherries. Bring to boil. Remove from heat; let stand 5 minutes. Using slotted spoon, transfer cherries to medium bowl.

Boil cooking liquid until reduced to 2 cups, about 25 minutes. Mix in orange peel, almond extract and nutmeg. Cool. Pour syrup over cherries; toss. Cover and refrigerate until cold. *(Can be made 1 day ahead. Keep refrigerated.)* Spoon cherry mixture into bowls and serve.

6 SERVINGS

fruit desserts

Rhubarb Napoleons

PASTRY

2   tablespoons ($^1/_4$ stick) unsalted butter
1   sheet frozen puff pastry (half of 17.3-ounce package), thawed
2   tablespoons sugar

FILLING

1   pound rhubarb, cut into $^1/_2$-inch pieces (about 3 cups)
$^2/_3$ cup sugar
2   tablespoons orange juice
1   tablespoon cornstarch
2   teaspoons grated orange peel
1   tablespoon red currant jelly

    Powdered sugar
1   pint vanilla ice cream
    Fresh mint sprigs (optional)

FOR PASTRY: Preheat oven to 400°F. Using $^1/_2$ tablespoon butter, generously butter 1 baking sheet. Unfold pastry on work surface; sprinkle with 2 tablespoons sugar. Roll out pastry to 11-inch square. Trim edges to form 10-inch square. Cut square into four 5-inch squares. Cut squares diagonally in half to form 8 triangles. Transfer triangles, sugar side up, to prepared baking sheet. Using remaining $1^1/2$ tablespoons butter, generously butter underside of second baking sheet. Place second sheet, buttered side down, atop pastry triangles.

Bake 15 minutes; press top baking sheet down to flatten. Bake until pastries are golden brown, about 10 minutes longer. Remove top baking sheet. Using metal spatula, transfer pastries to rack and cool.

FOR FILLING: Combine rhubarb, $^2/_3$ cup sugar, orange juice, cornstarch and grated orange peel in medium saucepan; stir to blend. Let stand until juices form, about 10 minutes. Cook over medium-high heat until rhubarb is tender but still intact, stirring gently, about 7 minutes. Gently stir in red currant jelly. Cool 5 minutes. *(Pastries and filling can be prepared 1 day ahead. Store pastries airtight at room temperature. Cover and refrigerate filling. Rewarm filling before using.)*

Arrange 1 pastry triangle on each of 4 plates; top with rhubarb filling, then remaining 4 pastry triangles. Sprinkle with powdered sugar. Scoop ice cream alongside each napoleon. Garnish with mint sprigs, if desired. Serve napoleons immediately.

4 SERVINGS

Fresh rhubarb is at its peak in the spring, so that's the perfect time to make this dessert. Use the bright red portions of the rhubarb stalks for the prettiest result. Be sure to butter the baking sheets generously to prevent sticking.

Fresh Pineapple Poached in Cinnamon Syrup

Note that this simple dessert can be prepared up to two days ahead of time. Serve the pineapple and syrup over vanilla ice cream or frozen yogurt, if desired.

1$^1/_2$ cups water
$^3/_4$ cup sugar
3   cinnamon sticks, broken in half
3   $^1/_4$-inch-thick slices peeled fresh ginger
1   $^1/_4$-inch-thick slice fresh lemon
1   large pineapple (about 4$^1/_2$ pounds), peeled, cored, cut into $^3/_4$-inch-thick pieces

Stir 1$^1/_2$ cups water and next 4 ingredients in large pot over medium heat until sugar dissolves. Bring to boil; cover and simmer 10 minutes to blend flavors. Add pineapple and simmer until just translucent, stirring occasionally, about 7 minutes. Transfer mixture to bowl. Chill until cold, at least 2 hours. *(Can be made 2 days ahead. Cover and keep chilled.)*

6 TO 8 SERVINGS

Strawberry and Peach Parfaits with Maple Granola

1$^1/_2$ cups old-fashioned oats
$^1/_4$ cup almonds, coarsely chopped
$^1/_4$ cup plus 3 tablespoons pure maple syrup
1$^1/_2$ teaspoons unsalted butter
$^1/_3$ cup raisins

3   cups sliced hulled strawberries (about 1$^1/_2$ one-pint baskets)
3   cups thinly sliced pitted peeled peaches (about 6 medium)
    Nonfat vanilla frozen yogurt (optional)

Preheat oven to 350°F. Mix oats and almonds in 13x9x2-inch baking dish. Combine $^1/_4$ cup syrup and butter in small saucepan. Bring to boil. Pour mixture over oat mixture; stir to blend. Bake 10 minutes, stirring occasionally. Add raisins; stir to blend. Bake until mixture is golden and crisp, stirring occasionally, about 8 minutes longer. Cool granola in dish. *(Can be made 1 week ahead. Store airtight at room temperature.)*

Gently toss strawberries, peaches and remaining 3 tablespoons maple syrup in large bowl to blend. Divide fruit mixture among 6 parfait glasses. Sprinkle each with granola, dividing equally. Top each with scoop of frozen yogurt, if desired, and serve.

6 SERVINGS

Baked Pears with Currants and Cinnamon

10 firm but ripe Comice or Anjou pears, unpeeled

$^2/_3$ cup sugar

$^2/_3$ cup (packed) dark brown sugar

$1^1/_2$ teaspoons ground cinnamon

$^2/_3$ cup dried currants

$^2/_3$ cup (or more) water

Top the pears with dollops of whipped cream, if desired. These would also be great served with madeleines from the bakery.

Preheat oven to 350°F. Using apple corer, cut through stem of each pear and all the way through pear to base to remove core. Trim bottoms so that pears stand straight. Arrange pears in 15x10x2-inch glass baking dish. Combine sugar, brown sugar and cinnamon in medium bowl. Add currants. Fill pear cavities with half of sugar mixture. Stir $^2/_3$ cup water into remaining sugar mixture; pour around pears. *(Can be prepared 8 hours ahead of time. Cover and refrigerate.)*

Bake pears uncovered until tender and sauce is syrupy, adding more water to dish by $^1/_4$ cupfuls if syrup becomes too thick and basting occasionally, about 50 minutes. Serve pears warm with syrup.

10 SERVINGS

Cherry and Apricot Cobbler

FILLING

2 pounds fresh Bing cherries, pitted, or two 1-pound bags frozen sweet cherries, thawed, drained

2 pounds apricots, halved, pitted

1 cup sugar

3 tablespoons cornstarch

1 teaspoon almond extract

TOPPING

2¹/₂ cups all purpose flour

¹/₂ cup plus 1 tablespoon sugar

1¹/₂ teaspoons baking powder

³/₄ teaspoon baking soda

¹/₂ teaspoon salt

¹/₂ cup (1 stick) chilled unsalted butter, cut into ¹/₂-inch cubes

³/₄ cup chilled buttermilk

³/₄ cup chilled whipping cream

Whipped cream or vanilla ice cream

FOR FILLING: Preheat oven to 400°F. Toss cherries, apricots, sugar, cornstarch and almond extract in large bowl to blend. Transfer to 13x9x2-inch glass baking dish. Bake until filling is hot and begins to bubble at edges, about 35 minutes. Reduce oven temperature to 375°F.

MEANWHILE, PREPARE TOPPING: Whisk flour, ¹/₂ cup sugar and next 3 ingredients in another large bowl to blend. Add butter; rub in with fingertips until mixture resembles coarse meal. Slowly add buttermilk and cream, tossing with fork until dough comes together.

Drop dough by rounded tablespoonfuls over hot filling to cover. Sprinkle with remaining 1 tablespoon sugar. Continue to bake cobbler until topping is golden and tester inserted into center of topping comes out clean, about 40 minutes. Cool 15 minutes. Serve cobbler warm with whipped cream or vanilla ice cream.

12 SERVINGS

Blueberry Crisp with
Walnut Streusel Topping

TOPPING

1¹/₂ cups all purpose flour

¹/₂ cup sugar

1 teaspoon grated lemon peel

1 teaspoon ground cinnamon

10 tablespoons (1¹/₄ sticks) chilled unsalted butter, cut into cubes

1 cup chopped walnuts

FILLING

8 cups fresh blueberries (about 2¹/₂ pounds)

³/₄ cup sugar

2 tablespoons fresh lemon juice

1¹/₂ tablespoons cornstarch

1¹/₂ teaspoons ground cinnamon

This classic warm-weather dessert takes almost no time to ready for baking. The fruit mixture gets made right in the baking dish.

FOR TOPPING: Whisk first 4 ingredients in bowl to blend. Add butter and rub in with fingertips, pressing until moist clumps form. Mix in nuts. *(Topping can be made 1 day ahead. Cover and chill.)*

FOR FILLING: Preheat oven to 375°F. Place blueberries in 13x9x2-inch glass baking dish or 3-quart round baking dish with 2-inch-high sides. Add sugar, lemon juice, cornstarch and cinnamon to berries; toss gently to blend. Spread berry mixture evenly in dish; sprinkle topping over. Bake until topping is brown and filling bubbles thickly, about 50 minutes. Cool.

6 TO 8 SERVINGS

Lemon-Blueberry Cake with White Chocolate Frosting

This cake can be prepared up to a day ahead of time. Cover it with a dome and refrigerate. Let stand at room temperature for about one hour before serving.

CAKE

3¹/₃ cups cake flour
¹/₂ teaspoon salt
¹/₂ teaspoon baking powder
¹/₂ teaspoon baking soda
³/₄ cup (1¹/₂ sticks) unsalted butter, room temperature
2 cups sugar
¹/₃ cup fresh lemon juice
1 teaspoon (packed) grated lemon peel
4 large eggs
1 cup plus 2 tablespoons buttermilk
2¹/₂ cups fresh blueberries

FROSTING

11 ounces good-quality white chocolate, finely chopped
12 ounces cream cheese, room temperature
³/₄ cup (1¹/₂ sticks) unsalted butter, room temperature
2 tablespoons fresh lemon juice

Additional blueberries (optional)
Lemon slices (optional)

FOR CAKE: Preheat oven to 350°F. Butter and flour two 9-inch-diameter cake pans with 2-inch-high sides; line bottoms with parchment.

Sift first 4 ingredients into medium bowl. Using electric mixer, beat butter in large bowl until fluffy. Gradually add sugar, beating until blended, scraping down sides of bowl. Beat in lemon juice and peel, then eggs 1 at a time. Continue to beat until well blended. Beat in dry ingredients in 4 additions alternately with buttermilk. Fold in berries. Transfer to pans. Bake until tester comes out clean, about 40 minutes. Cool in pans on racks.

FOR FROSTING: Stir white chocolate in top of double boiler set over barely simmering water until almost melted. Remove from over water and stir until smooth. Cool to lukewarm. Beat cream cheese and butter in large bowl until blended. Beat in lemon juice, then cooled white chocolate.

Turn cakes out onto work surface. Peel off parchment. Place 1 cake layer, flat side up, on platter. Spread with 1 cup frosting. Top with second cake layer, flat side down. Spread remaining frosting over top and sides of cake. Garnish with additional blueberries and lemon slices, if desired.

10 TO 12 SERVINGS

cakes

Orange Cheesecake with Caramel Sauce

For a pretty garnish, make crystallized orange slices. Begin by slicing an orange paper-thin, leaving the rind intact. Remove any seeds. Bring two cups of water and one cup of sugar to a boil. Add orange slices to syrup and simmer 10 minutes. Transfer to rack and let dry one hour. Sprinkle orange slices with sugar and place atop cheesecake.

CRUST

11	whole graham crackers, broken
1/4	cup sugar
5	tablespoons unsalted butter, melted

FILLING

4	8-ounce packages cream cheese, room temperature
1 1/3	cups sugar
6	large eggs
3	tablespoons orange liqueur
5	teaspoons finely grated orange peel
2	teaspoons vanilla extract
	Caramel Sauce (see recipe below)

FOR CRUST: Preheat oven to 350°F. Finely grind crackers and sugar in processor. Add butter; process until crumbs are moist. Press onto bottom of 9-inch-diameter springform pan with 2 1/2-inch-high sides. Bake until set, 12 minutes. Transfer to rack; cool. Maintain oven temperature.

FOR FILLING: Using electric mixer, beat cream cheese and sugar in large bowl until smooth. Beat in next 4 ingredients. Pour filling atop crust in pan.

Bake until cake is puffed, outer 2-inch edge is set and center moves just slightly when shaken, about 1 hour 10 minutes. Transfer cake to rack. Run knife around pan sides to loosen; cool 1 hour. Chill cheesecake overnight (or up to 2 days). Serve with sauce.

8 TO 10 SERVINGS

Caramel Sauce

2	cups sugar
1/2	cup water
3/4	cup whipping cream
3	tablespoons orange liqueur

Stir sugar and 1/2 cup water in medium saucepan over medium-low heat until sugar dissolves. Increase heat; boil without stirring until syrup turns deep amber, brushing down sides of pan with wet pastry brush and swirling pan, 9 minutes. Remove from heat. Add cream (mixture will bubble vigorously). Stir over low heat until smooth. Remove from heat. Whisk in liqueur.

MAKES ABOUT 1 3/4 CUPS

Pound Cake with Fresh Fruit and Bourbon Whipped Cream

      3   cups all purpose flour
    1/2   teaspoon baking soda
    1/2   teaspoon salt
      3   cups sugar
      1   cup (2 sticks) unsalted butter, room temperature
      4   large eggs
      1   tablespoon vanilla extract
      1   cup buttermilk

          Powdered sugar
          Lightly sweetened sliced fresh fruit (such as hulled strawberries, nectarines,
            plums and grapes)
          Bourbon Whipped Cream (see recipe below)

Preheat oven to 350°F. Butter and flour 10x4-inch angel food cake pan. Sift flour, baking soda and salt into small bowl. Using electric mixer, beat 3 cups sugar and butter in large bowl until blended. Add eggs 1 at a time, beating after each addition. Beat in vanilla. Add flour mixture alternately with buttermilk in 3 additions each, beating just until blended after each addition. Transfer batter to prepared pan.

Bake cake until tester inserted near center comes out clean, about 1 hour 20 minutes. Cool cake in pan on rack 20 minutes. Run knife around pan sides and center tube to loosen. Turn out onto rack and cool. *(Can be made 1 day ahead. Cover; store at room temperature.)*

Sift powdered sugar over cake. Serve with fruit and whipped cream.

12 SERVINGS

Bourbon Whipped Cream

      2   cups chilled whipping cream
      6   tablespoons golden brown sugar
      3   tablespoons bourbon

Combine all ingredients in medium bowl and beat to soft peaks.

MAKES ABOUT 3 1/2 CUPS

Move over, Margarine

It used to be a common belief that margarine was more healthful than butter. Dutiful home cooks, in the name of nutrition, used margarine instead of butter as a spread—and to cook and bake with. Today we know that while margarine has less cholesterol than butter, it contains trans fatty acids, which have recently been associated with elevated cholesterol levels. The calorie count of the two products is the same, approximately 100 calories per tablespoon. In a taste test, though, butter always comes out ahead. Its sweet, mellow flavor and creamy texture will convert even the most dedicated margarine users.

Even though old habits die hard, margarine, to many foodies, is a thing of the past. Chefs today not only insist on using butter, many are devotees of Plugrá, a European-style butter available in specialty foods stores that is higher in fat than American brands. As the American Butter Institute's John Whetten said: "I'd rather trust a cow than a chemist." So would we.

Chocolate Crunch Layer Cake
with Milk Chocolate Frosting

When making the frosting, quickly cool down the melted chocolate mixture by whisking it over ice.

Beat the cooled chocolate with a handheld mixer until the color lightens and the frosting is thick enough to form soft peaks when the beaters are removed.

CAKE

    4 ounces unsweetened chocolate

$^1/_2$ cup hot water

$1^3/_4$ cups cake flour

    1 teaspoon baking soda

$^1/_2$ teaspoon salt

$^1/_2$ cup (1 stick) unsalted butter, room temperature

$1^3/_4$ cups sugar

    3 large eggs, room temperature

    1 teaspoon vanilla extract

$^2/_3$ cup whole milk

FROSTING

$1^1/_4$ cups whipping cream

$^1/_4$ cup light corn syrup

$^1/_4$ cup ($^1/_2$ stick) unsalted butter

    1 pound milk chocolate, chopped

    4 1.4-ounce chocolate-covered English toffee bars (such as Heath or Skor), cut into $^1/_4$-inch pieces

    1 7-ounce milk chocolate bar (such as Hershey's)

FOR CAKE: Position rack in center of oven and preheat to 350°F. Butter two 9-inch-diameter cake pans with $1^3/_4$-inch-high sides. Line pans with waxed paper; butter paper. Dust pans with flour; tap out excess. Combine chocolate and $^1/_2$ cup hot water in small saucepan. Stir over low heat until melted and smooth. Cool to lukewarm, stirring often.

Whisk flour, baking soda and salt in medium bowl to blend. Using electric mixer, beat butter in large bowl until fluffy. Gradually beat in sugar. Beat in eggs 1 at a time, then vanilla. Beat in chocolate mixture. Add flour mixture in 3 additions alternately with milk in 2 additions, beating just to blend after each addition. Divide batter between pans.

Bake cakes until tester inserted into center comes out clean and cake just begins to pull away from sides of pan, about 35 minutes. Cool cakes in pans on racks 5 minutes. Cut around pan sides. Turn cakes out onto racks; peel off waxed paper. Cool cakes completely.

FOR FROSTING: Combine cream, corn syrup and butter in heavy large saucepan. Whisk over medium heat until mixture begins to simmer. Add

Some frosting topped with a generous sprinkling of diced English toffee bars makes up the filling between the cake layers.

Spread a thin layer of frosting, called the crumb coat, over the cake to anchor any crumbs and provide a smooth surface for the final coat of frosting.

chocolate. Reduce heat to low and whisk until smooth, about 1 minute; transfer chocolate mixture to bowl.

Fill another large bowl with ice. Set bottom of bowl with frosting atop ice. Whisk until frosting is cool and begins to thicken, about 8 minutes. Place bowl of frosting on work surface. Using electric mixer, beat until color lightens and soft peaks form when beaters are lifted, about 2 minutes (frosting will continue to thicken as it stands).

Place 1 cake layer, flat side up, on 8-inch-diameter tart pan bottom or cardboard round. If desired, place pan bottom with cake atop 8-inch-diameter cake pan to make simple decorating stand. Top layer with 1½ cups frosting, spreading to edge. Sprinkle evenly with diced toffee. Top with second cake layer, flat side down; press slightly to adhere. Spread thin layer of frosting over top and sides of cake to seal and set crumbs. Spread remaining frosting over top and sides of cake.

Stand chocolate bar on 1 short end. Using vegetable peeler and starting at top edge of 1 side, run peeler down length of bar (chocolate will come away from side of chocolate bar in curls). Pile chocolate curls atop cake. Chill at least 2 hours. *(Can be made 2 days ahead. Cover with cake dome and keep chilled. Let stand at room temperature 1 hour before serving.)*

10 TO 12 SERVINGS

Raspberry-Apricot Shortcakes

The Cinnamon Biscuits (there are a couple extra) would also be great on their own, topped with butter and jam, at breakfast or for a snack.

2 pounds apricots (about 12), pitted, cut into $1/3$-inch-thick wedges
1 cup sugar
1 cup plus 1 tablespoon water

1 teaspoon unflavored gelatin
$1^1/_4$ cups chilled whipping cream
$1/_4$ cup powdered sugar

10 warm Cinnamon Biscuits (see recipe opposite)
2 $1/_2$-pint baskets fresh raspberries

Place apricots in large bowl. Combine 1 cup sugar and 1 cup water in small saucepan. Bring to boil, stirring until sugar dissolves. Mix sugar syrup into apricots. Cool completely.

Place 1 tablespoon water in small cup. Sprinkle unflavored gelatin over. Let stand until gelatin softens, about 5 minutes. Set cup in 1-inch-deep simmering water in medium saucepan; stir until gelatin dissolves, about 3 minutes. Remove from heat. Using electric mixer, beat cream and powdered sugar in large bowl just until mixture thickens. Gradually add warm gelatin mixture, beating until medium-firm peaks form. *(Apricots and*

cream can be prepared 8 hours ahead. Cover separately and refrigerate.)

Cut biscuits horizontally in half. Place 1 biscuit bottom in each of 10 shallow bowls. Spoon apricots with some syrup over bottoms. Top with whipped cream, raspberries and biscuit tops. Drizzle remaining syrup from apricots around shortcakes and serve.

10 SERVINGS

Cinnamon Biscuits

$^2/_3$ cup plus 2 tablespoons sugar
 2 cups all purpose flour
 2 cups cake flour
 4 teaspoons baking powder
$^3/_4$ teaspoon salt
$^1/_2$ teaspoon ground cinnamon
$^1/_4$ teaspoon baking soda
$^3/_4$ cup (1$^1/_2$ sticks) chilled unsalted butter, cut into $^1/_2$-inch cubes
 2 large eggs
 1 cup chilled plain yogurt

Blend $^2/_3$ cup sugar, all purpose flour, cake flour, baking powder, salt, cinnamon and baking soda in large bowl. Add butter; rub in with fingertips until mixture resembles coarse meal. Beat eggs in medium bowl. Transfer 1 tablespoon beaten eggs to small bowl; reserve for glaze. Whisk yogurt into remaining eggs in medium bowl. Stir yogurt mixture into dry ingredients. Gather dough into ball.

Gently knead dough on lightly floured surface until dough just holds together, about 6 turns. Roll or pat dough into 1-inch-thick round. Using 2$^1/_2$- to 3-inch-diameter heart-shape cookie cutter, cut out biscuits. Gather dough scraps, reroll to 1-inch thickness and cut out additional biscuits. Place biscuits on ungreased baking sheet. *(Can be made 1 day ahead. Cover biscuits and egg glaze separately and refrigerate.)*

Preheat oven to 400°F. Brush biscuits with egg glaze. Sprinkle with remaining 2 tablespoons sugar. Bake biscuits until puffed and light golden, about 18 minutes. Cool 10 minutes. Serve warm or at room temperature.

MAKES ABOUT 12

Wedding Shower Dinner for Ten

Chilled Cream of Corn Soup
(page 204)

Roasted Sea Bass with Tomato Coulis and Fennel Salsa
(page 92)

Potato Salad with Olives, Beans and Red Onion
(page 140)

Roasted Asparagus

Champagne

Raspberry-Apricot Shortcakes
(opposite; pictured opposite)

Pistachio-topped Flan

Make this luscious flan the day before a dinner party and serve it straight from the refrigerator.

Nonstick vegetable oil spray
1 cup sugar
3 tablespoons water

6 large eggs
³/4 teaspoon vanilla extract
Pinch of salt
1¹/2 cups whole milk
1¹/2 cups whipping cream

¹/3 cup chopped pistachios

Preheat oven to 350°F. Spray 9-inch-diameter cake pan with 2-inch-high sides with nonstick spray. Combine ²/3 cup sugar and 3 tablespoons water in heavy small saucepan. Stir over medium heat until sugar dissolves. Increase heat and boil without stirring until syrup is deep amber, occasionally brushing down sides of pan with pastry brush dipped into water and swirling pan, about 10 minutes. Immediately pour caramel into prepared cake pan. Using pot holders to protect hands from hot caramel, rotate pan to coat bottom (not sides) of pan. Cool.

Whisk remaining ¹/3 cup sugar, eggs, vanilla and salt in medium bowl to blend. Whisk in milk and cream. Pour custard mixture through sieve into caramel-lined pan. Place pan with custard in roasting pan. Pour enough hot water into roasting pan to come halfway up sides of cake pan.

Bake custard until center no longer moves when pan is gently shaken and knife inserted into center comes out clean, about 1 hour. Remove custard from roasting pan. Cool 15 minutes. Chill uncovered until cold, at least 6 hours or overnight.

Run small knife between pan and custard to loosen. Place platter atop custard. Firmly hold pan and platter together and invert, shaking gently to unmold custard onto platter. Sprinkle custard with pistachios.

6 TO 8 SERVINGS

mousses & puddings

Coffee Mousse

1	cup sugar
$1/2$	cup all purpose flour
$41/2$	teaspoons instant espresso powder
5	large egg yolks
2	cups whole milk
$11/2$	cups chilled whipping cream
	Whole coffee beans (optional)

Whisk sugar, flour and instant espresso powder in heavy medium saucepan to blend. Whisk in egg yolks. Gradually whisk in milk. Whisk mixture over medium heat until very thick and starting to boil, about 8 minutes. Transfer mixture to medium bowl. Press plastic wrap directly onto surface of mixture. Refrigerate until cold, about 1 hour.

Using electric mixer, beat 1 cup chilled whipping cream in medium bowl until stiff peaks form. Whisk $1/4$ of whipped cream into espresso mixture to lighten. Fold remaining whipped cream into espresso mixture. Divide mousse equally among 6 wineglasses. Refrigerate 1 hour. *(Can be made up to 1 day ahead. Cover with plastic and keep refrigerated.)*

Beat remaining $1/2$ cup whipping cream in medium bowl to stiff peaks. Pipe or spoon whipped cream atop mousse in each wineglass. Garnish mousse with whole coffee beans, if desired, and serve.

6 SERVINGS

Hot Lemon Soufflés

$1/2$	cup (1 stick) unsalted butter
$3/4$	cup sugar
$1/2$	cup fresh lemon juice
$21/2$	teaspoons finely minced lemon peel
4	large eggs, separated

Butter six $3/4$-cup ramekins; dust with sugar. Melt $1/2$ cup butter in heavy medium saucepan over medium-low heat. Add sugar and stir until mixture is opaque, about 2 minutes. Stir in lemon juice and lemon peel. Whisk in yolks. Cook over medium-low heat until mixture thickens and thermometer registers 180°F, whisking constantly, about 12 minutes (do not boil). Transfer to large bowl; cool to room temperature, 30 minutes.

Position rack in center of oven and preheat to 400°F. Using electric mixer, beat egg whites in another large bowl until stiff but not dry. Fold 1/4 of beaten egg whites into lemon mixture to lighten. Fold remaining beaten egg whites into lemon mixture.

Divide mixture among prepared ramekins. Place ramekins in large roasting pan. Fill pan with enough hot water to come halfway up sides of ramekins. Bake soufflés until golden brown on top, about 14 minutes. Using tongs, remove soufflés from water and serve immediately.

MAKES 6

Caramelized Mango-Lime Tapioca

3³/₄ cups whole milk

³/₄ cup sugar

¹/₃ cup quick-cooking tapioca

2 large eggs

1¹/₂ teaspoons finely grated lime peel

¹/₄ teaspoon salt

1 teaspoon vanilla extract

1 ripe mango, peeled, pitted, diced (about 1 cup)

16 teaspoons golden brown sugar

Running this moist pudding under the broiler for a few minutes causes the brown sugar topping to melt into a sweet syrup.

Stir milk, sugar, tapioca, eggs, lime peel and salt in heavy medium saucepan to blend. Let stand 5 minutes. Stir over medium-high heat until mixture thickens and just comes to boil, about 10 minutes. Transfer pudding to large bowl. Lay plastic wrap directly on surface of pudding and cool to lukewarm. Mix in vanilla. *(Can be prepared 1 day ahead. Cover and refrigerate. Stir to loosen before continuing.)*

Preheat broiler. Divide mango among eight ³/₄-cup ramekins. Spoon pudding atop mango, dividing equally. Smooth tops with spatula. Sprinkle 2 teaspoons brown sugar evenly over each pudding. Let stand until sugar begins to melt, 10 minutes. Place ramekins on baking sheet. Broil until sugar bubbles all over, watching closely and turning frequently, 4 minutes. Serve puddings warm.

8 SERVINGS

Chocolate Pots de Crème with White Chocolate Whipped Cream

2 cups whipping cream
4 ounces semisweet chocolate, chopped
1 teaspoon instant espresso powder or coffee powder
6 large egg yolks
3 tablespoons sugar

White Chocolate Whipped Cream (see recipe below)

Position rack in center of oven and preheat to 325°F. Arrange six ³/₄-cup custard cups or soufflé dishes in roasting pan. Combine whipping cream, chopped semisweet chocolate and instant espresso powder in heavy medium saucepan. Bring almost to simmer over medium heat, whisking until chocolate melts and mixture is smooth. Whisk egg yolks and sugar in large bowl to blend. Gradually whisk in hot cream mixture.

Divide custard equally among cups. Pour enough hot water into pan to come halfway up sides of cups. Bake custards until just set around edges but still soft in center, about 25 minutes. Remove cups from water. Refrigerate uncovered until cold, at least 2 hours. *(Can be made 1 day ahead. Cover with plastic wrap and keep refrigerated.)*

Spoon White Chocolate Whipped Cream atop custards and serve.

6 SERVINGS

White Chocolate Whipped Cream

2 ounces good-quality white chocolate (such as Lindt or Baker's), chopped
2 tablespoons plus ¹/₂ cup chilled whipping cream

Combine chopped white chocolate and 2 tablespoons whipping cream in small metal bowl. Set over small saucepan of simmering water and stir until white chocolate melts and mixture is smooth. Remove bowl from over water. Cool white chocolate mixture 10 minutes.

Beat remaining ¹/₂ cup chilled whipping cream in medium bowl until soft peaks form. Whisk in white chocolate mixture. *(Can be prepared 1 day ahead. Cover with plastic wrap and refrigerate.)*

MAKES ABOUT 1 CUP

Coconut Crème Brûlée

- $^1/_2$ cup plus 6 teaspoons sugar
- 6 large egg yolks
- 1 large egg
- 2 cups whipping cream
- $^2/_3$ cup unsweetened canned coconut milk*
- $^2/_3$ cup flaked sweetened coconut

Preheat oven to 350°F. Place six $^3/_4$-cup custard cups in large roasting pan. Whisk $^1/_2$ cup sugar, yolks and whole egg in large bowl to blend. Combine cream, coconut milk and coconut in heavy medium saucepan. Bring to boil. Whisk into yolk mixture. Pour custard into cups, dividing equally.

Pour enough hot water into roasting pan to come halfway up sides of cups. Bake until custards are just set in center, about 35 minutes. Remove from water. Cool; chill overnight.

Preheat broiler. Arrange custard cups on baking sheet. Sprinkle 1 teaspoon sugar evenly over each. Broil until sugar browns, rotating baking sheet for even browning and watching closely, about 2 minutes. Refrigerate custards at least 1 hour and up to 6 hours before serving.

Coconut milk is available at Indian, Southeast Asian and Latin American markets and many supermarkets nationwide.

6 SERVINGS

Bring out the Blowtorch

Long ago, pastry chefs who wanted to produce a quickly caramelized surface for crème brûlée (burnt cream) would pass a salamander, a blazing-hot cast iron disk on a long iron rod, over a layer of sugar granules until they melted and browned. The task grew easier when the dessert was instead placed beneath a preheated broiler. But both techniques still held the possibility of uneven caramelization.

To the rescue came handheld butane-fueled torches, which produce a focused flame that provides maximum precision and intense heat that melts the sugar quickly while the food beneath it remains cool. Chefs working in volume use large models. Now, however, home cooks can buy smaller-scale butane torches in kitchenware and specialty stores. Look for butane-fueled models that feature adjustable flames and safe, comfortable grips.

Bear in mind that such utensils are tailored to the very specific task of melting sugar. A broiler works well enough for the occasional crème brûlée maker. For the best results when using a broiler, place the individual ramekins or custard cups on a baking sheet, place under the broiler, and watch carefully, occasionally rotating the baking sheet for even browning.

Frozen Milk Chocolate and Amaretto Mousse Pie

This pie must be frozen for at least four hours (and as long as overnight), so begin preparing it some time before you plan to serve it. Note that milk chocolate is used in this recipe; dark chocolate reacts differently in recipes, so don't use the two interchangeably.

26 chocolate wafer cookies
1/4 cup (1/2 stick) unsalted butter, melted
9 ounces milk chocolate, finely chopped
1/3 cup amaretto
1/4 cup light corn syrup
1 1/2 cups chilled whipping cream

Preheat oven to 350°F. Butter 9-inch-diameter glass pie dish. Finely grind cookies in processor. Add melted butter; blend until moist crumbs form. Press crumbs onto bottom and up sides of pie dish. Bake until crust is set, about 12 minutes. Cool on rack.

Stir chocolate and amaretto in medium metal bowl set over saucepan of simmering water until chocolate is melted and smooth (do not allow bottom of bowl to touch water). Remove bowl from over water. Stir in corn syrup. Cool to room temperature.

Beat cream in large bowl to soft peaks. Fold 1/4 of whipped cream into chocolate mixture, then fold in remaining cream. Spoon filling into crust. Freeze until firm, at least 4 hours or overnight.

8 TO 10 SERVINGS

Hot Fudge-Peppermint Sundaes

frozen desserts

1 12-ounce package semisweet chocolate chips
1/2 cup (1 stick) unsalted butter
1/2 cup whipping cream
1/3 cup sugar
1 teaspoon vanilla extract
Pinch of salt
2 pints vanilla ice cream
15 hard red-and-white-striped peppermint candies, crushed

Combine first 4 ingredients in heavy medium saucepan. Stir over low heat until melted and smooth. Remove from heat. Stir in vanilla and salt. *(Can be made 2 weeks ahead. Cover; chill. Rewarm before using.)*

Place 2 scoops ice cream in each of 6 sundae glasses. Spoon hot fudge sauce over ice cream. Sprinkle with crushed peppermint candies.

6 SERVINGS

Chocolate-Cherry Ice Cream Bombe

1 16-ounce jar purchased hot fudge sauce
1 12-ounce package semisweet chocolate chips
3 tablespoons water
$^1/_4$ cup brandy

3 pints cherry-vanilla ice cream with chocolate chunks or fudge flakes, slightly softened
$1^1/_2$ pints chocolate sorbet or chocolate-cherry sorbet, slightly softened
1 9-ounce package chocolate wafer cookies

Stir first 3 ingredients in heavy medium saucepan over medium-low heat until melted and smooth. Remove from heat. Whisk in brandy. Cool.

Line 10-inch-diameter, 10-cup metal bowl with plastic wrap, extending over sides. Spread cherry-vanilla ice cream over inside of bowl to within $^3/_4$ inch of top edge, leaving center 6-inch-diameter hollow. Freeze 30 minutes. Fill hollow completely with sorbet; smooth top. Overlap half of cookies (about 22) atop ice cream and sorbet, covering completely and pressing gently. Spread $1^1/_3$ cups fudge sauce over cookies. Overlap remaining cookies atop sauce. Cover; freeze bombe overnight. Cover and chill remaining sauce. *(Can be made 3 days ahead. Keep bombe frozen and sauce chilled.)*

Rewarm remaining sauce over low heat. Turn bombe out onto platter. Peel off plastic. Cut into wedges and serve with sauce.

12 TO 16 SERVINGS

Dress up this dessert by topping it with chocolate curls and maraschino cherries. It's very impressive, yet surprisingly easy to make.

Vacherins with Raspberry Sorbet and Mixed Berry-Cardamom Sauce

Fold down the top two inches of a large pastry bag to form a collar. Holding the pastry bag underneath the collar, use a large spatula to fill the bag approximately 3/4 full with meringue.

Twist the top of the bag to close it, then grasp the top with one hand and position the other hand a couple of inches above the tip. Push out the meringue by squeezing the top of the bag. Using the lower hand to guide the bag and starting in the center of one marked circle, pipe the meringue in a continuous spiral; fill the circle to form the base of the *vacherin*.

MERINGUES

1¹/₂ cups sugar

2 tablespoons cornstarch

6 large egg whites, room temperature

¹/₄ teaspoon cream of tartar

SAUCE

³/₄ cup seedless raspberry jam

¹/₂ cup sugar

¹/₃ cup water

1 16-ounce package frozen unsweetened mixed berries (do not thaw)

1 teaspoon ground cardamom

3 pints raspberry sorbet
Fresh raspberries
Fresh mint sprigs

FOR MERINGUES: Position 1 rack in bottom third and 1 rack in top third of oven; preheat to 200°F. Line 2 large baking sheets with parchment paper. Using 3¹/₄- to 3¹/₂-inch-diameter cookie cutter as template, heavily trace 4 circles on each parchment sheet. Turn parchment over so that marked side faces down (circles will show through).

Whisk sugar and cornstarch in medium bowl to blend. Using heavy-duty or handheld electric mixer on medium-high speed, beat whites in large bowl until foamy, about 1 minute. Add cream of tartar; beat until soft peaks form, about 1 minute. Add sugar mixture, 1 tablespoon at a time, beating until whites are very stiff and glossy, at least 4 minutes with heavy-duty mixer and 6 to 8 minutes with handheld. Scoop enough meringue into pastry bag fitted with medium star tip to fill ³/₄ full. Pipe small dot of meringue under parchment paper in each corner of baking sheets. Press parchment onto dots.

Starting in center of 1 marked circle, pipe meringue in continuous spiral to fill circle completely. Pipe 1 meringue circle atop edge of base circle, forming standing rim. Repeat, piping 2 more circles atop first, forming meringue cup. Pipe 3 more cups on sheet, filling bag with meringue as needed. Pipe 4 cups on second sheet.

Bake meringues 3 hours without opening oven door (sides of meringues may settle slightly). Turn off oven; let meringues stand in closed oven overnight to dry. *(Can be made 1 week ahead. Store airtight in single layer.)*

To build up the vacherin, pipe three circles of meringue, one on top of another, around the edge of the base circle. Begin each circle about one inch from the end of the last.

FOR SAUCE: Whisk raspberry jam, sugar and $^1/_3$ cup water in heavy medium saucepan over medium-high heat until sugar dissolves and jam melts. Boil until sauce thickens and is reduced to generous $^3/_4$ cup, whisking often, about 7 minutes. Add frozen mixed berries and cardamom; stir gently. Remove from heat; let stand 1 hour. Cover; chill at least 2 hours and up to 1 day.

Scoop raspberry sorbet into vacherins. Spoon sauce over. Garnish with fresh raspberries and mint. Serve with remaining sauce.

8 SERVINGS

A Surplus of Egg Whites

Some desserts, such as custards and ice creams, call for a lot of egg yolks—which means a lot of leftover egg whites. Fortunately, egg whites can be refrigerated for four days or frozen up to a year. When thawed in the refrigerator, they should beat up to the same volume as fresh egg whites, so you'll be able to use them in soufflés, meringues, angel food cakes and any other recipes that call for egg whites. Don't forget, too, that egg whites can be scrambled or made into omelets on their own for healthful breakfast dishes.

To store egg whites, carefully separate the eggs, making sure no bits of yolk remain in the whites. Transfer the egg whites to a container. They can be frozen together in one container; or frozen singly in ice cube trays, then turned out and sealed in a plastic bag to save having to measure the whites for future recipes. To use the whites, thaw them overnight in the refrigerator. If necessary, measure two tablespoons of thawed egg white for each fresh egg white in the recipe.

Cinnamon-Clove Ice Cream

- 2 cups whole milk
- 2 cups whipping cream
- 1 cup sugar
- 6 whole cinnamon sticks
- 16 whole cloves, slightly crushed
- 8 large egg yolks

Combine milk, cream, $1/2$ cup sugar, cinnamon and cloves in heavy medium saucepan. Bring to boil over medium-high heat, stirring until sugar dissolves. Remove from heat. Cover; steep 1 hour.

Whisk yolks and $1/2$ cup sugar in large bowl to blend. Bring milk mixture to simmer. Gradually whisk into yolk mixture; return to pan. Stir over medium-low heat until custard thickens (do not boil). Strain into medium bowl; chill uncovered until cold, stirring occasionally, 2 hours.

Process chilled custard in ice cream maker according to manufacturer's instructions. Transfer ice cream to container; cover and freeze.

MAKES ABOUT 5 CUPS

Tropical Bananas Foster

- $1/4$ cup ($1/2$ stick) butter
- $1/2$ cup (packed) dark brown sugar
- $1/4$ cup mango nectar
- 1 tablespoon dark rum
- 1 tablespoon minced crystallized ginger
- $1/8$ teaspoon ground nutmeg
- 1 cup diced peeled pineapple
- 1 banana, peeled, sliced
- 1 cup diced peeled mango
  Vanilla ice cream or macadamia brittle ice cream
  Toasted sweetened coconut

Melt butter in large skillet over medium heat. Add next 3 ingredients; stir until sugar dissolves. Increase heat and boil until syrupy, 4 minutes. Mix in ginger and nutmeg. Add all fruit; sauté until heated through, 1 minute. Cool slightly. Scoop ice cream into bowls. Spoon sauce over. Sprinkle with toasted coconut. Serve immediately.

6 SERVINGS

The Flavors of Bon Appétit 2001

Oatmeal Cookie Sandwiches with Nectarine Ice Cream

COOKIES

$1^1/_2$ cups old-fashioned oats

$^3/_4$ cup all purpose flour

$^1/_2$ teaspoon baking soda

$^1/_2$ teaspoon ground cinnamon

$^1/_4$ teaspoon salt

$^1/_2$ cup (1 stick) unsalted butter, room temperature

$^1/_3$ cup (packed) dark brown sugar

$^1/_3$ cup sugar

 1 large egg

$^1/_2$ teaspoon vanilla extract

ICE CREAM

   Nonstick vegetable oil spray

$1^1/_2$ pounds nectarines, pitted, cut into $^1/_4$-inch cubes

$^1/_4$ cup sugar

 1 pint vanilla ice cream, slightly softened

FOR COOKIES: Position 1 rack in top third and 1 rack in bottom third of oven; preheat to 350°F. Line 2 baking sheets with parchment paper.

Mix first 5 ingredients in medium bowl. Using electric mixer, beat butter in large bowl until fluffy. Add both sugars; beat until well blended. Beat in egg and vanilla. Stir in dry ingredients. Using 2 tablespoons batter per cookie, drop 8 mounds onto each sheet, spacing apart. Flatten to 2-inch rounds.

Bake 10 minutes. Reverse baking sheets and bake until cookies are golden and dry to touch, about 3 minutes longer. Cool 2 minutes. Transfer to rack. Cool completely. (*Can be made 1 day ahead. Store airtight.*)

FOR ICE CREAM: Preheat oven to 375°F. Spray rimmed baking sheet with nonstick spray. Spread nectarines in single layer on sheet. Sprinkle with sugar; toss to coat. Bake 15 minutes. Stir well. Bake until fruit is tender and juices begin to thicken and caramelize, stirring every 5 minutes, about 20 minutes longer. Transfer fruit and juices to large bowl; mash coarsely; cool. Mix ice cream into fruit. Freeze until almost firm, about 45 minutes.

Place 8 cookies, flat side up, on work surface. Spread $^1/_3$ cup ice cream over each. Top each with 1 cookie, flat side down, and press gently to adhere (reserve any remaining ice cream for another use). Wrap sandwiches in foil and freeze. (*Can be made 3 days ahead. Keep frozen.*)

MAKES 8 SANDWICHES

Cookies-and-Cream Ice Cream Cake

1 16-ounce pound cake, thawed if frozen
6 cups cookies-and-cream ice cream (from $1/2$ gallon), slightly softened

1 16-ounce jar purchased hot fudge sauce
1 12-ounce package semisweet chocolate chips
$1/4$ cup water
10 Oreo cookies, coarsely chopped

1 cup chilled whipping cream
3 tablespoons sugar
   Assorted candies (such as M&M's, gumdrops and candy sprinkles)

Cut cake into $1/3$-inch-thick slices. Halve each slice diagonally, forming triangles. Cover bottom of 9-inch-diameter springform pan with cake by arranging some triangles, points facing in, around edge of pan. Fill in center with more triangles; then cut additional pieces to fill in any spaces. Spread half of ice cream over cake. Freeze until firm, about 1 hour.

Stir fudge sauce, chocolate chips and $1/4$ cup water in heavy medium saucepan over medium-low heat until melted and smooth. Cool to barely lukewarm. Spread half of fudge sauce over ice cream. Sprinkle with chopped cookies. Top with enough remaining cake slices to cover. Spread remaining ice cream over. Freeze 1 hour.

Stir remaining fudge sauce in saucepan over medium-low heat until barely lukewarm. Pour sauce over ice cream, spreading to edge. Freeze at least 6 hours or overnight.

Beat cream and sugar in medium bowl to peaks. Run knife around pan sides to loosen cake. Release pan sides. Spread whipped cream around sides (not top) of cake. *(Can be made 1 day ahead. Freeze.)* Arrange candies atop.

10 TO 12 SERVINGS

Grand Marnier Brownie Kisses

Espresso and a selection of favorite liqueurs are good with these very grown-up brownies.

BROWNIES

4 ounces unsweetened chocolate, chopped

$^1/_2$ cup (1 stick) unsalted butter

$1^1/_4$ cups sugar

2 teaspoons grated orange peel

1 teaspoon vanilla extract

$^1/_4$ teaspoon salt

3 large eggs

$^3/_4$ cup all purpose flour

TOPPING

$^1/_2$ cup whipping cream

1 teaspoon grated orange peel

$5^1/_2$ ounces bittersweet (not unsweetened) or semisweet chocolate, chopped

3 tablespoons Grand Marnier or other orange liqueur

FOR BROWNIES: Preheat oven to 325°F. Line 8x8-inch metal baking pan with foil. Melt unsweetened chocolate and butter in heavy medium saucepan over low heat, stirring until smooth; cool slightly. Whisk sugar, orange peel, vanilla and salt into chocolate mixture. Whisk in eggs 1 at a time, then continue whisking until mixture is velvety. Add flour and whisk just to blend. Transfer batter to prepared pan.

Bake brownies until top is just springy to touch and toothpick inserted into center comes out with moist crumbs attached, about 35 minutes. Cool in pan on rack 10 minutes. If necessary, press down on raised brownie edges to level top. Cool in pan completely.

FOR TOPPING: Bring cream and orange peel to simmer in heavy small saucepan. Remove from heat. Add chocolate and whisk until smooth. Whisk in Grand Marnier. Refrigerate until thick enough to spread, stirring occasionally, about 45 minutes.

Spread topping over brownies. Refrigerate until topping is cold, about 1 hour. *(Can be made 1 week ahead. Cover tightly and keep refrigerated.)* Using foil as aid, lift brownies from pan; trim edges. Cut into 25 squares. Let stand at room temperature 30 minutes before serving.

MAKES 25

cookies

Chocolate Chunk, Orange and Hazelnut Cookies

$1^1/_4$ cups all purpose flour

$^1/_2$ teaspoon baking soda

$^1/_8$ teaspoon salt

$^3/_4$ cup (packed) golden brown sugar

$^1/_2$ cup (1 stick) unsalted butter, room temperature

4 teaspoons grated orange peel

1 teaspoon vanilla extract

1 large egg

3 3-ounce bars bittersweet chocolate, cut into $^1/_3$-inch chunks

$1^1/_2$ cups hazelnuts (about 6 ounces), toasted, husked, chopped

Preheat oven to 375°F. Combine flour, baking soda and $^1/_8$ teaspoon salt in medium bowl; whisk to blend. Using electric mixer, beat brown sugar, butter, grated orange peel and vanilla extract in large bowl until light and fluffy. Beat in egg. Add flour mixture and mix just until combined. Mix in chocolate chunks and toasted hazelnuts.

Drop batter by heaping tablespoonfuls onto 2 ungreased baking sheets, spacing 2 inches apart. Bake cookies until just firm to touch and beginning to brown, about 13 minutes. Transfer to racks; cool. *(Can be made 2 days ahead. Store airtight at room temperature.)*

MAKES ABOUT 24

A steaming mug of hot chocolate or a glass of milk would complement these updated, sophisticated chocolate chip cookies nicely.

Honey, Anise and Almond Biscotti

      2 cups all purpose flour
      1 teaspoon baking powder
$^1/_2$ teaspoon baking soda
$^1/_2$ teaspoon salt
$^1/_2$ cup vegetable oil
$^1/_2$ cup sugar
$^1/_2$ cup honey
      2 large eggs
      2 teaspoons grated lemon peel
      2 teaspoons aniseed, crushed
      1 teaspoon vanilla extract
$1^1/_2$ cups slivered almonds (about 6 ounces), lightly toasted

Whisk flour, baking powder, baking soda and salt in medium bowl to blend. Whisk oil, sugar, honey, eggs, lemon peel, aniseed and vanilla in large bowl until smooth. Stir in flour mixture, then nuts. Cover and refrigerate dough until well chilled, about 3 hours.

Preheat oven to 350°F. Butter and flour 2 large baking sheets. Spoon dough in 3 equal strips (2 on one sheet, spaced apart, and 1 on second sheet). Using floured hands, shape strips into 2-inch-wide by 1-inch-high logs.

Bake logs until just springy to touch, switching and turning pans after 10 minutes, about 20 minutes total (logs will spread). Cool 15 minutes on sheets. Maintain oven temperature.

Using large spatula, gently transfer logs to work surface. Using serrated knife, cut each log on diagonal into $^1/_2$-inch-thick slices. Arrange slices, cut side down, on baking sheets. Bake until bottom side browns, about 7 minutes. Turn cookies over. Bake until bottom side browns, 7 minutes longer. Transfer to racks and cool (cookies will crisp as they cool). *(Can be made 2 weeks ahead. Store airtight at room temperature.)*

MAKES ABOUT 48

Afternoon Tea for Twelve

Assorted Cheeses and Crackers

Cucumber Sandwiches

Orange and Cream Scones
    (page 152)

Clotted Cream

Honey, Anise and Almond
    Biscotti
        (at left; pictured opposite)

Milk Chocolate-Espresso Truffles
    (page 218)

Black and Herbal Teas

Ginger Spice Cookies

2 cups all purpose flour
$2^1/2$ teaspoons ground ginger
2 teaspoons baking soda
1 teaspoon ground cinnamon
1 teaspoon ground cloves
$3/4$ teaspoon salt
$3/4$ cup chopped crystallized ginger
1 cup (packed) dark brown sugar
$1/2$ cup vegetable shortening, room temperature
$1/4$ cup ($1/2$ stick) unsalted butter, room temperature
1 large egg
$1/4$ cup mild-flavored (light) molasses
   Sugar

Combine first 6 ingredients in medium bowl; whisk to blend. Mix in crystallized ginger. Using electric mixer, beat brown sugar, shortening and butter in large bowl until fluffy. Add egg and molasses; beat until blended. Add flour mixture and mix just until blended. Cover; chill 1 hour.

Preheat oven to 350°F. Lightly butter 2 baking sheets. Spoon sugar in thick layer onto small plate. Using wet hands, form dough into $1^1/4$-inch balls; roll in sugar to coat completely. Place balls on prepared baking sheets, spacing 2 inches apart.

Bake cookies until cracked on top but still soft to touch, about 12 minutes. Cool on sheets 1 minute. Carefully transfer to racks and cool. *(Can be made 5 days ahead. Store airtight at room temperature.)*

MAKES ABOUT 30

Cherry-Almond Bars

1¹/₂   cups all purpose flour

¹/₄   cup cornstarch

¹/₈   teaspoon salt

³/₄   cup (1¹/₂ sticks) unsalted butter, room temperature

¹/₂   cup sugar

1   teaspoon vanilla extract

¹/₄   teaspoon almond extract

³/₄   cup coarsely chopped toasted slivered almonds (about 3 ounces)

1¹/₄   cups cherry preserves

The easy thing about bar cookies is that they don't require dropping dough onto cookie sheets and baking multiple batches; simply press the dough into a pan, bake and cut into bars for serving.

Preheat oven to 350°F. Line 11x7-inch glass baking dish with foil. Combine first 3 ingredients in medium bowl; whisk to blend. Using electric mixer, beat butter in large bowl until light and fluffy. Add sugar and beat until light. Beat in vanilla and almond extracts. Add flour mixture and beat just until dough begins to come together. Mix in almonds. Press dough onto bottom of prepared dish. Pierce all over with fork. Bake until just firm to touch, about 45 minutes.

Stir preserves in small saucepan over medium-low heat until melted and hot; spread over warm pastry. Bake until preserves bubble in center, about 15 minutes. Cool in dish on rack.

Using foil as aid, lift entire cookie from dish; trim edges. Cut into 2x1-inch bars. *(Can be made 2 days ahead. Cover and chill.)*

MAKES 30

White Chocolate and Strawberry
Cheesecake (page 210)

How America Eats

The votes are in! In our annual "How America Eats" survey, we asked readers to rate their favorite foods. Then we found recipes that made the most of the top ten winners. Those recipes, which run the gamut from soups to desserts, appear here—two for each favored food, asparagus to strawberries, cheese to chocolate.

Farfalle with Asparagus, Roasted Shallots and Blue Cheese

Asparagus is in the lead as America's favorite vegetable, capturing 51 percent of the vote. This is its second year as a survey winner, an achievement that didn't extend to the "least favorite vegetable" category—okra earned that title this year; cabbage won "least favorite" last year.

1¹/₂ pounds medium shallots (about 24), peeled, halved lengthwise
4 tablespoons olive oil

1 cup fresh breadcrumbs made from French bread

1¹/₂ pounds farfalle (bow-tie) pasta
2 pounds thin asparagus, trimmed, cut diagonally into 1¹/₂-inch pieces
1 pound creamy blue cheese (such as Saga blue or Gorgonzola), cut into ¹/₂-inch pieces

Preheat oven to 375°F. Toss shallots with 2 tablespoons oil on baking sheet; spread in single layer. Sprinkle with salt and pepper. Bake until tender and golden brown, stirring occasionally, about 35 minutes.

Stir 2 tablespoons oil and breadcrumbs in skillet over medium heat until crumbs brown, about 4 minutes. *(Shallots and crumbs can be made 8 hours ahead. Cover separately; keep at room temperature.)*

Cook pasta in large pot of boiling salted water 10 minutes. Add asparagus; cook until asparagus is crisp-tender and pasta is tender but still firm to bite, about 4 minutes. Drain pasta and asparagus. Transfer to large bowl. Immediately add blue cheese and shallots. Toss until cheese melts. Season with salt and pepper. Sprinkle with breadcrumbs.

6 SERVINGS

Warm Asparagus and Prosciutto Salad

asparagus

3 ounces thinly sliced prosciutto

1¹/₄ pounds asparagus, trimmed

3 tablespoons plus ¹/₂ cup olive oil
2 anchovy fillets, chopped
3 garlic cloves, thinly sliced
¹/₃ cup fresh lemon juice

1 5-ounce package mixed baby greens (about 10 cups)
Farinata Wedges (see recipe opposite)

Preheat oven to 350°F. Line baking sheet with parchment paper. Place prosciutto slices in single layer on parchment. Bake until crisp, about 18 minutes. Cool. Break prosciutto into bite-size pieces.

Meanwhile, cook asparagus in heavy large pot of boiling salted water until crisp-tender, about 4 minutes. Drain. Transfer asparagus to bowl filled with ice water to cool. Drain thoroughly.

Heat 3 tablespoons oil in large nonstick skillet over medium heat. Add anchovies and garlic and sauté until garlic is golden, about 1 minute. Add asparagus and prosciutto and sauté until heated through, about 3 minutes. Add lemon juice and remaining 1/2 cup oil and simmer 1 minute. Remove from heat. Season to taste with salt and pepper.

Divide mixed baby greens among 6 plates. Top with asparagus mixture, dividing equally. Pour dressing from skillet over each serving. Serve warm with Farinata Wedges.

6 SERVINGS

Farinata Wedges

    2 cups (8³/₄ ounces) chickpea flour*
1¹/₄ teaspoons salt
 ³/₄ teaspoon ground pepper
1³/₄ cups water, room temperature
 ¹/₄ cup plus 2 tablespoons olive oil

Whisk chickpea flour, salt and pepper in large bowl to blend. Whisk 1³/₄ cups water and ¹/₄ cup olive oil in medium bowl. Add water mixture to dry ingredients; whisk until batter is smooth. Cover and let batter stand at room temperature 1 hour.

Preheat broiler. Coat 12-inch-diameter ovenproof skillet with 1 tablespoon olive oil. Pour half of batter into skillet, tilting skillet to spread evenly. Broil until golden brown, about 4 minutes. Reduce oven temperature to 450°F. Transfer skillet to oven and bake farinata until knife inserted into center comes out clean, about 3 minutes. Cool. Run spatula around sides of skillet to loosen farinata, then slide out onto cutting board. Repeat with second half of batter. Cut each farinata into 6 wedges.

Available at Middle Eastern markets and some natural foods stores.

6 SERVINGS

Bon Appétit readers really like to cook. An impressive majority of them (78 percent) make a main course for dinner three times a week or more.

Noodles with Pesto, Parmesan and Broccoli

Broccoli came in second among favorite vegetables, with 32 percent of the vote. It shows up here in a quick and easy pasta dish and in a broccoli stir-fry with tofu (which signals another trend: 70 percent sometimes eat vegetarian entrées; half of those do so once a week).

1   16-ounce package wide egg noodles

1/4   cup olive oil
1   large onion, chopped
3   garlic cloves, chopped
1/2   teaspoon dried crushed red pepper
8   cups broccoli florets (from about 4 large stalks)
1   cup grated Parmesan cheese
3/4   cup purchased pesto

Cook noodles in large pot of boiling salted water until tender but still firm to bite. Drain noodles, reserving 1 cup cooking liquid.

Heat olive oil in heavy large pot over medium heat. Add onion, garlic and dried red pepper and sauté until onion is translucent, about 5 minutes. Add broccoli and 1/4 cup reserved noodle cooking liquid. Cover pot and cook until broccoli is crisp-tender, about 4 minutes. Add noodles, 1/2 cup Parmesan cheese and pesto. Toss until noodles are evenly coated, adding remaining reserved liquid by tablespoonfuls if mixture is dry. Season to taste with salt and pepper. Transfer mixture to large bowl. Sprinkle with remaining 1/2 cup Parmesan cheese.

4 TO 6 SERVINGS

Broccoli, Mushroom and Bell Pepper Stir-fry with Tofu

broccoli

6   tablespoons olive oil
8   ounces firm tofu, well drained, cut into 1/2-inch cubes
2   tablespoons minced peeled fresh ginger
3   garlic cloves, minced
1   pound fresh shiitake mushrooms, stems trimmed, caps sliced
2   cups broccoli florets
2   red bell peppers, cut into strips
2   bunches green onions, cut into 1-inch pieces
1/2   cup sake or dry white wine
1/4   cup soy sauce
1   tablespoon oriental sesame oil

Heat 3 tablespoons olive oil in large nonstick skillet or wok over high heat. Add tofu; stir gently until starting to brown around edges, about 4 minutes. Using slotted spoon, transfer to bowl. Add 3 tablespoons oil, ginger and garlic to skillet; stir 1 minute. Add mushrooms; stir-fry until tender and golden around edges, about 5 minutes. Add broccoli, bell peppers and green onions; stir-fry until vegetables are crisp-tender, about 3 minutes. Return tofu to skillet; stir to mix. Stir in sake, soy sauce and sesame oil; simmer 1 minute. Season with salt and pepper. Transfer to large bowl and serve.

4 SERVINGS

Survey repondents like to experiment in the kitchen—especially when entertaining. More than one in four readers say they always experiment with new recipes when people come over, and 68 percent try out new dishes on unsuspecting guests at least some of the time.

Chilled Cream of Corn Soup

Corn is the last of the top three vegetables; 26 percent call it their favorite. Try it in this sophisticated chilled soup with white truffle oil or in our new-fangled version of the picnic classic—potato salad with corn and chilies for spice.

8 large ears corn, husked
2 tablespoons ($^1/_4$ stick) butter
$^2/_3$ cup minced shallots
6 cups water
$^1/_4$ cup dry white wine

1 cup half and half

1 tablespoon chopped fresh chives
1 tablespoon white truffle oil* (optional)

Cut corn kernels from cobs. Melt butter in heavy large pot over medium heat. Add shallots and sauté until tender, about 3 minutes. Add corn kernels, 6 cups water and white wine. Bring mixture to boil. Reduce heat; simmer 2 minutes. Cool 10 minutes.

Working in batches, puree soup in blender. Strain through fine sieve into large bowl. Cool. Add half and half. Season to taste with salt and pepper. Refrigerate at least 4 hours. *(Soup can be prepared 2 days ahead. Cover and keep refrigerated.)*

Ladle soup into bowls. Sprinkle with chives. Drizzle oil over, if desired.

Available at Italian markets, specialty foods stores and some supermarkets.

10 SERVINGS

Potato Salad with Chilies and Corn

corn

2 medium poblano chilies*
1 yellow bell pepper
$1^1/_2$ cups fresh or frozen corn kernels
2 cups diced seeded tomatoes
3 green onions, thinly sliced
$^1/_4$ cup chopped fresh cilantro
1 teaspoon minced seeded jalapeño chili

$1^1/_2$ pounds small red-skinned new potatoes, cut in half, halves cut into $^1/_4$-inch-thick slices
2 garlic cloves

3 tablespoons fresh lime juice
2 tablespoons olive oil

1 bunch watercress, thick stems trimmed

Char poblano chilies and bell pepper over gas flame or in broiler until blackened on all sides. Enclose in plastic bag; let stand 10 minutes. Peel and seed chilies and bell pepper; cut into ¼-inch pieces. Transfer to large bowl. Cook corn in medium saucepan of boiling salted water until crisp-tender, about 5 minutes. Drain. Mix corn, tomatoes, green onions, cilantro and jalapeño into chili-bell pepper mixture.

Cook potatoes in large pot of boiling salted water 5 minutes. Add garlic and continue boiling until potatoes are just tender, about 3 minutes longer. Drain. Rinse potatoes and garlic under cold water to cool. Drain. Mince garlic. Mix potatoes and garlic into chili-bell pepper mixture.

Whisk lime juice and olive oil in small bowl to blend. Add to potato mixture; toss to coat. Season to taste with salt and pepper. *(Can be made 1 day ahead. Cover and refrigerate.)*

Arrange watercress around edge of platter; mound potato salad in center.

Fresh green chilies, often called pasillas; *available at Latin American markets and also at some supermarkets nationwide.*

6 TO 8 SERVINGS

Women readers place greater emphasis on romance than men do, particularly when it comes to the importance of candlelight (40 percent versus 23 percent) and flowers (39 percent versus 20 percent). No real news here.

Gruyère and Parsley Omelets

4 large eggs

3 tablespoons chopped fresh Italian parsley

2 teaspoons water

1 teaspoon dried fines herbes or dried salad herbs

1/4 teaspoon salt

1/4 teaspoon ground black pepper

2 tablespoons (1/4 stick) butter

1/2 cup (packed) grated Gruyère cheese (about 2 ounces)

Beat eggs, 2 tablespoons parsley, 2 teaspoons water, dried herbs, salt and pepper in small bowl to blend. Melt 1 tablespoon butter in small nonstick skillet over medium-high heat. Add half of egg mixture (about 1/2 cup) to skillet. Cook until eggs are just set in center, tilting pan and lifting edge of omelet with spatula to let uncooked portion flow underneath, about 2 minutes. Top half of omelet with 1/4 cup cheese. Using spatula, fold other half of omelet over cheese; slide out onto plate. Repeat with remaining butter, egg mixture and cheese. Sprinkle omelets with remaining 1 tablespoon parsley and serve immediately.

2 SERVINGS

Grilled Cheddar, Tomato and Bacon Sandwiches

cheese

8 thick-cut bacon slices

8 slices country-style sourdough bread or batard (cut on deep diagonal into 5x3x1/2-inch slices)

2 cups (packed) grated extra-sharp cheddar cheese (about 8 ounces)

8 tomato slices, seeds removed, slices drained on paper towels

4 tablespoons mayonnaise

Cook bacon in heavy large skillet over medium heat until brown and crisp, turning occasionally, about 6 minutes. Transfer bacon to paper towels and drain. Wash and dry skillet.

Place 4 bread slices on work surface. Press 1/4 cup grated cheese onto each slice. Top each with 2 tomato slices. Sprinkle with pepper. Place 2 bacon slices atop each, breaking into pieces if necessary to fit. Press

^{1}/4 cup grated cheese over bacon on each. Top sandwiches with remaining bread slices, then spread ^{1}/2 tablespoon mayonnaise over top of each.

Heat 2 heavy large skillets over medium heat. Add 2 sandwiches, mayonnaise side down, to each skillet. Place plate atop both sandwiches to weigh down. Cook sandwiches until bottom is golden brown, about 2 minutes. Spread top of each sandwich with ^{1}/2 tablespoon mayonnaise. Turn sandwiches over, mayonnaise side down. Top with plates and cook until golden brown on bottom, about 2 minutes. Transfer sandwiches to work surface. Cut sandwiches crosswise in half and serve.

4 SERVINGS

Bon Appétit readers are a hospitable bunch, entertaining friends or relatives (on average) 2.3 times a month.

Spaghetti Carbonara

Pasta tied for first place in the comfort foods category, with 26 percent calling it their favorite. (Ice cream also came in first with 26 percent of the vote.) So if you're feeling in need of a little comfort, try either of these great pasta preparations.

9   bacon slices, chopped
1   tablespoon butter
$^1/_2$ cup whipping cream
$^1/_2$ cup grated Parmesan cheese
4   large egg yolks

12   ounces spaghetti
     Additional grated Parmesan cheese

Combine bacon and butter in heavy large skillet over medium heat. Sauté until bacon is brown and crisp. Using slotted spoon, transfer bacon to paper towels and drain. Whisk cream, $^1/_2$ cup grated cheese and egg yolks in medium bowl to blend; whisk in 2 tablespoons drippings from skillet. Set cream mixture aside; discard remaining drippings.

Cook pasta in large pot of boiling salted water until tender but still firm to bite, stirring occasionally. Drain pasta and return to same pot. Add cream mixture to pasta. Toss over medium-low heat until sauce cooks through and coats pasta thickly, about 4 minutes (do not boil). Mix in bacon. Season to taste with salt and pepper. Divide pasta among plates. Serve, passing additional cheese separately.

2 TO 4 SERVINGS

Garlicky Linguine with Crab, Red Bell Pepper and Pine Nuts

pasta

5   tablespoons unsalted butter
1   red bell pepper, finely chopped
4   garlic cloves, finely chopped
$^1/_4$ teaspoon dried crushed red pepper
$^1/_2$ cup dry white wine

12   ounces linguine

1   8-ounce bottle clam juice
1   pound fresh lump crabmeat, picked over
$^1/_4$ cup finely chopped fresh parsley
$^1/_3$ cup pine nuts, toasted
     Freshly grated Parmesan cheese

Melt butter in heavy large skillet over medium heat. Add red bell pepper; cover and cook 2 minutes. Add garlic and dried red pepper; cover and cook 2 minutes. Increase heat to high, add white wine and boil 2 minutes. Set mixture aside.

Cook pasta in large pot of boiling salted water until tender but still firm to bite. Drain pasta, reserving $1/2$ cup cooking water.

Return pasta to pot. Add clam juice, $1/2$ cup cooking water and bell pepper mixture. Cook over high heat until pasta absorbs half of liquid, about 2 minutes. Add crabmeat and toss until heated through, about 1 minute. Mix in parsley. Season to taste with pepper. Divide pasta among bowls. Sprinkle with pine nuts. Serve, passing cheese separately.

4 SERVINGS

White Chocolate and
Strawberry Cheesecake

Strawberries are the favorite fruit of 39 percent who responded to our survey. Eat them plain, dusted with powdered sugar, or use them to add a special touch to desserts, as in this white chocolate cheesecake and *panna cotta*, a simple Italian custard made with cream.

CRUST

1 9-ounce package chocolate wafer cookies, broken into pieces

¹/₂ cup (1 stick) unsalted butter, melted

FILLING

1 pound good-quality white chocolate (such as Lindt or Baker's), finely chopped

4 8-ounce packages cream cheese, room temperature

1 cup sugar

¹/₄ teaspoon salt

4 large eggs

1 cup sour cream

¹/₂ cup whipping cream

2 tablespoons vanilla extract

3 1-pint baskets strawberries, hulled, halved

¹/₂ cup apricot preserves

2 tablespoons brandy

FOR CRUST: Position rack in center of oven; preheat to 325°F. Butter 10-inch-diameter springform pan. Wrap outside of pan with foil. Finely grind cookies in processor. Add melted butter; process until crumbs are moist. Press crumbs onto bottom and 2 inches up sides of pan. Bake until set, about 15 minutes. Cool on rack. Maintain oven temperature.

FOR FILLING: Stir chocolate in double boiler over barely simmering water until melted. Remove; cool to lukewarm, stirring. Using electric mixer, beat cream cheese in large bowl until fluffy. Add sugar, then salt; beat until smooth. Add eggs 1 at a time, beating well after each addition. Add sour cream, whipping cream and vanilla; beat until well blended. Gradually add melted white chocolate, beating until smooth. Pour into crust.

Bake cake until top begins to brown but center still moves slightly when pan is gently shaken, about 1 hour 20 minutes. Open oven door slightly; turn off oven. Leave cake in oven 30 minutes. Chill cake uncovered overnight. *(Can be made 2 days ahead. Cover; keep refrigerated.)*

Run small knife between pan sides and cake. Release pan sides. Starting at outer edge of top of cake, arrange strawberry halves in slightly overlapping concentric circles, covering top completely. Stir preserves and brandy in small saucepan over medium heat until mixture boils. Strain. Brush glaze over strawberries.

12 TO 14 SERVINGS

strawberries

Buttermilk Panna Cotta with Sweetened Strawberries

1/3 cup plus 6 tablespoons sugar

2 tablespoons water

2 cups whipping cream

1 1/2 teaspoons unflavored gelatin

1/2 vanilla bean, split lengthwise

1 cup buttermilk

1 16-ounce basket strawberries, hulled, sliced (about 3 cups)

1/4 cup (packed) golden brown sugar

Place six 3/4-cup custard cups on small baking sheet. Combine 1/3 cup sugar and 2 tablespoons water in heavy small saucepan. Stir over medium-low heat until sugar dissolves. Increase heat and boil without stirring until syrup turns deep amber, occasionally brushing down sides of pan with wet pastry brush and swirling pan, about 8 minutes. Immediately pour caramel into custard cups, dividing equally; tilt cups to cover bottoms (caramel layer will be thin). Cool until set.

Pour 1/4 cup cream into small bowl; sprinkle gelatin over. Let stand until gelatin softens, about 10 minutes. Combine remaining 6 tablespoons sugar and remaining 1 3/4 cups cream in heavy medium saucepan. Scrape in seeds from vanilla bean; add bean. Bring just to simmer. Remove from heat. Add gelatin mixture and whisk until gelatin dissolves. Strain mixture into 4-cup glass measuring cup. Whisk in buttermilk. Divide mixture among caramel-lined custard cups. Refrigerate panna cotta uncovered overnight. *(Can be made 2 days ahead. Cover and keep refrigerated.)*

Toss strawberries and brown sugar in large bowl. Let stand until juices form, about 30 minutes and up to 2 hours.

Run knife between panna cotta and custard cups to loosen. Invert onto plates. Using rubber spatula, scrape any caramel remaining on bottom of cups over panna cotta. Spoon strawberries alongside and serve.

6 SERVINGS

Fruit, just fruit, is a popular dessert among readers, but 62 percent expand those horizons once or twice a week and make something special to have after dinner.

Almond-Raspberry Clafoutis

Raspberries came in second for favorite fruit, with an impressive 31 percent of the vote. As good as they are out of hand, raspberries shine in this beautiful tart and in these *clafoutis*—a classic French dessert of fruit baked in a custard or cake batter. This version is cakier than some you might have had.

ॐ

1 10-ounce package frozen raspberries in syrup, thawed
1 cup (4$^1/_2$ ounces) whole almonds, toasted
1$^1/_2$ cups sugar
7 large egg whites
$^3/_4$ cup all purpose flour
$^1/_4$ cup orange juice
1 tablespoon grated orange peel

1 cup (2 sticks) unsalted butter
2 $^1/_2$-pint baskets fresh raspberries

Puree frozen raspberries with syrup in processor until smooth. *(Raspberry sauce can be prepared 1 day ahead. Cover and refrigerate.)*

Preheat oven to 350°F. Finely grind almonds in processor. Transfer ground almonds to large bowl. Add sugar, egg whites, flour, orange juice and orange peel and whisk to blend well.

Melt butter in heavy medium saucepan over medium heat; cook until butter browns, stirring frequently, about 4 minutes. Whisk hot browned butter into almond batter until well blended. Divide batter equally among six 1$^1/_4$-cup custard cups (batter will fill cups only halfway). Drop 8 fresh raspberries into batter in each cup.

Bake until golden brown and set in center, 40 minutes. Cool 15 minutes. Garnish with any remaining raspberries. Serve warm with sauce.

MAKES 6

Raspberry-Crème Fraîche Tart

raspberries

$^1/_2$ cup (1 stick) unsalted butter, room temperature
$^3/_4$ cup plus 2 tablespoons sugar
$^1/_4$ teaspoon salt
4 large eggs
1 teaspoon vanilla extract
1 cup all purpose flour

$^3/_4$ cup crème fraîche*
2 cups fresh raspberries
Powdered sugar

Place baking sheet in bottom of oven. Preheat oven to 375°F. Wrap outside of 11-inch-diameter tart pan with removable bottom with foil. Using electric mixer, beat butter, $1/2$ cup sugar and salt in large bowl until blended. Add 3 eggs and $1/2$ teaspoon vanilla extract; beat until smooth. Add flour; beat just until blended. Spread batter over bottom and $1/2$ inch up sides of prepared pan.

Beat $1/4$ cup sugar, 1 egg, $1/2$ teaspoon vanilla and crème fraîche in bowl until well blended. Spread custard over batter. Arrange berries $1/4$ inch apart atop custard. Sprinkle tart with 2 tablespoons sugar.

Bake until set and brown around edges, 45 minutes. Cool. *(Can be made 1 day ahead. Cover loosely with foil; chill. Serve at room temperature.)*

Remove pan sides. Place tart on platter. Dust with powdered sugar.

*Crème fraîche is available at some supermarkets.

8 TO 10 SERVINGS

Berries may have been big winners this year, but their numbers couldn't top the total brought in by the *least* favorite fruit: Figs captured 47 percent of that vote, with kiwi a distant second at 17 percent.

Peach Pie with Lattice Crust

Peaches, with 29 percent calling them their favorite fruit, nearly tied with raspberries at the number two spot in that category. In the summer, when they're in season, there's no getting enough of them. That's the time to make these two recipes.

peaches

CRUST

$2^1/_2$ cups all purpose flour
1 tablespoon sugar
2 teaspoons ground ginger
2 teaspoons ground cinnamon
$^1/_2$ teaspoon salt
10 tablespoons ($1^1/_4$ sticks) chilled unsalted butter, cut into $^1/_2$-inch cubes
$^1/_2$ cup chilled solid vegetable shortening, cut into pieces
4 tablespoons (or more) ice water

FILLING

$^2/_3$ cup (packed) golden brown sugar
$^1/_4$ cup cornstarch
1 teaspoon fresh lemon juice
$^1/_2$ teaspoon ground ginger
$^1/_2$ teaspoon ground cinnamon
3 pounds medium peaches

FOR CRUST: Whisk first 5 ingredients in medium bowl to blend. Add butter and shortening and rub in with fingertips until mixture resembles very coarse meal. Mix in 4 tablespoons ice water. Mix in more water by tablespoonfuls if dough is dry, tossing until moist clumps form. Gather dough into ball. Divide into 2 pieces, 1 slightly larger than the other. Flatten into disks; wrap and chill at least 2 hours and up to 2 days.

FOR FILLING: Mix brown sugar, cornstarch, lemon juice, ginger and cinnamon in large bowl. Bring medium saucepan of water to boil. Drop in 3 peaches at a time; blanch 1 minute. Transfer peaches to bowl of cold water. Using small sharp knife, peel 1 peach. Cut peach in half; discard pit and slice thinly. Stir peach slices into sugar mixture. Repeat with remaining peaches. Let filling stand until juices form, at least 30 minutes and up to 1 hour.

Preheat oven to 375°F. Roll out larger dough disk on lightly floured surface to 13- to 14-inch round. Transfer to 9-inch-diameter deep-dish pie dish. Roll out smaller dough disk on lightly floured surface to 11-inch round. Using ruler as aid, cut dough into $^1/_2$-inch-wide strips.

Spoon filling into dough-lined dish. Arrange some of dough strips atop pie, spacing $^3/_4$ inch apart. Form lattice by arranging more dough strips at right angle to first strips, spacing $^3/_4$ inch apart. Trim overhang of bottom crust and lattice strips to $^3/_4$ inch. Fold under and crimp edge.

Bake pie until crust is golden and filling bubbles thickly, covering edge of crust with foil if browning too quickly, about 1 hour 20 minutes. Cool pie to room temperature before serving.

8 SERVINGS

Spiced Peach Sundaes

$^1/_4$ cup ($^1/_2$ stick) unsalted butter

6   tablespoons (packed) dark brown sugar

1   teaspoon vanilla extract

$^1/_2$ teaspoon ground cardamom

$^1/_8$ teaspoon ground nutmeg

$2^1/_2$ pounds ripe peaches, pitted, cut into $^1/_4$-inch-thick slices

$^1/_2$ gallon vanilla ice cream
    Whole pecans, toasted
    Sweetened whipped cream

When asked where they get their recipes, readers declared their allegiance to cookbooks (90 percent) and admitted to a penchant for experimentation (49 percent).

Melt butter in heavy large skillet over medium heat. Add brown sugar; stir to blend. Add vanilla, cardamom and nutmeg. Stir 1 minute. Add peaches; toss gently to coat. Cook until sugar mixture melts and peaches are tender but do not fall apart, tossing occasionally, about 5 minutes. *(Can be made 8 hours ahead. Cover; chill. Rewarm over low heat.)*

Place 2 scoops ice cream in each of 8 bowls. Spoon peach mixture over ice cream, dividing equally. Garnish with pecans and whipped cream.

8 SERVINGS

Caramelized Pineapple with Brown Sugar-Ginger Ice Cream

Ice cream shares the number one spot in the comfort foods category with pasta; both won 26 percent of our reader vote. In a pinch, a plain bowl of ice cream will do. For an even more comforting dessert, make a homemade batch flavored with brown sugar and ginger, or use purchased ice cream to its best advantage in an irresistible cake.

1 pineapple, peeled, halved lengthwise, cored, each half cut lengthwise into 9 wedges

1 cup (packed) dark brown sugar

Brown Sugar-Ginger Ice Cream (see recipe below)

6 tablespoons sweetened flaked coconut, toasted

Preheat broiler. Line large baking sheet with foil. Arrange pineapple wedges side by side in single layer on prepared baking sheet. Pat pineapple wedges with paper towels to remove excess moisture. Using fingertips, press 1 cup brown sugar through coarse sifter over pineapple. Broil pineapple wedges until brown sugar caramelizes, watching closely to avoid burning and rotating baking sheet to broil evenly, about 3 minutes.

Arrange 3 wedges of warm pineapple in triangle on each of 6 plates. Place scoop of Brown Sugar-Ginger Ice Cream in center of each pineapple triangle. Sprinkle 1 tablespoon coconut over each and serve.

6 SERVINGS

Brown Sugar-Ginger Ice Cream

4 large egg yolks

6 tablespoons (packed) dark brown sugar

2 tablespoons sugar

Pinch of salt

$1^1/_4$ cups whipping cream

1 cup whole milk

1 teaspoon vanilla extract

$^1/_2$ teaspoon ground ginger

ice cream

Whisk yolks, both sugars and salt in medium bowl to blend. Bring cream and milk to simmer in medium saucepan. Gradually whisk hot cream mixture into yolk mixture. Return to saucepan. Stir over medium-low heat until custard thickens and leaves path on back of spoon, about 5 minutes (do not boil). Transfer custard to medium bowl. Whisk in vanilla and ginger. Chill at least 4 hours or overnight.

Process custard in ice cream maker according to manufacturer's instructions. Transfer ice cream to covered container and freeze.

6 SERVINGS

S'mores Coffee-Fudge Ice Cream Cake

16 whole graham crackers (about 8 ounces)
1 cup whole almonds, toasted
3 tablespoons sugar
$1/_2$ cup (1 stick) unsalted butter, melted

$1^1/_2$ quarts coffee ice cream, softened until spreadable
Fudge Sauce (see recipe below)

1 7-ounce jar marshmallow creme
2 cups miniature marshmallows

Preheat oven to 350°F. Finely grind graham crackers, almonds and sugar in processor. Add butter; process until moist crumbs form. Press mixture onto bottom and up sides of 9-inch-diameter springform pan with $2^3/_4$-inch-high sides. Bake until edges are golden, 12 minutes. Cool.

Spread 2 cups ice cream in crust. Spoon $3/_4$ cup cooled Fudge Sauce over. Freeze until just set, 10 minutes. Refrigerate or freeze remaining ice cream to prevent melting. Repeat layering with 2 cups ice cream, then $3/_4$ cup sauce. Freeze until just set. Spread remaining 2 cups ice cream over. Cover and freeze cake overnight. Chill remaining sauce.

Preheat broiler. Warm remaining sauce in small saucepan over low heat. Remove from heat. Place cake in pan on baking sheet. Spread marshmallow creme over top. Sprinkle marshmallows over in single layer. Broil just until marshmallows are brown, watching closely to avoid burning, 1 minute. Run knife around pan sides to loosen. Remove pan sides. Cut cake into wedges. Serve immediately with warm sauce.

10 TO 12 SERVINGS

Fudge Sauce

1 cup whipping cream
$1/_2$ cup light corn syrup
10 ounces bittersweet (not unsweetened) or semisweet chocolate, chopped

Bring cream and corn syrup to boil in heavy medium saucepan. Remove from heat. Add chocolate; whisk until melted and smooth. Chill sauce until cool but still pourable, stirring occasionally, about 45 minutes.

MAKES ABOUT $2^1/_2$ CUPS

Milk Chocolate-Espresso Truffles

Chocolate turned up as a favorite twice in our survey—it came in second as a favorite ice cream flavor, and chocolate chip cookies won a whopping 47 percent of the vote in the favorite cookie category. Chocoholics will love the fact that a whole pound of this ingredient is used in each of these recipes.

16 ounces milk chocolate, finely chopped
1/2 cup whipping cream
2 teaspoons instant espresso powder or instant coffee powder
2 tablespoons Kahlúa

1 cup (about) unsweetened cocoa powder

Stir first 3 ingredients in top of double boiler set over simmering water until smooth. Remove from over water. Whisk in Kahlúa. Cool 15 minutes. Freeze until firm, about 2 hours.

Line baking sheet with foil. Place cocoa powder on plate. Scoop chocolate mixture by very generously mounded teaspoonfuls onto prepared sheet, forming 1-inch mounds. Dust hands with cocoa powder; roll mounds between palms, forming smooth balls, then roll in cocoa powder to coat lightly. Return to sheet. Cover with foil and refrigerate truffles until firm, at least 2 hours. *(Can be made ahead. Chill in covered container up to 1 week or freeze up to 1 month.)* Let stand at room temperature until slightly softened before serving.

MAKES ABOUT 40

Giant Chocolate-Toffee Cookies

1/2 cup all purpose flour
1 teaspoon baking powder
1/4 teaspoon salt
16 ounces bittersweet (not unsweetened) or semisweet chocolate, chopped
1/4 cup (1/2 stick) unsalted butter

1 3/4 cups (packed) brown sugar
4 large eggs
1 tablespoon vanilla extract
5 1.4-ounce chocolate-covered English toffee bars (such as Heath), coarsely chopped (do not use English toffee bits)
1 cup walnuts, toasted, chopped

chocolate

Combine flour, baking powder and salt in bowl; whisk to blend. Stir chocolate and butter in top of double boiler set over simmering water until melted and smooth. Remove from over water. Cool to lukewarm.

Using electric mixer, beat sugar and eggs in bowl until thick, about

5 minutes. Beat in chocolate mixture and vanilla. Stir in flour mixture, then toffee and nuts. Chill batter until firm, about 45 minutes.

Preheat oven to 350°F. Line 2 large baking sheets with parchment or waxed paper. Drop batter by ¼ cupfuls onto sheets, spacing 2½ inches apart. Bake just until tops are dry and cracked but cookies are still soft to touch, about 15 minutes. Cool cookies on sheets. *(Can be prepared 2 days ahead. Store airtight at room temperature.)*

MAKES ABOUT 18

Digging for more than winners and losers, the survey sought to uncover why readers cook (other than simply to sustain themselves). "A sense of satisfaction" was the answer provided by 72 percent of respondents.

Index

Page numbers in *italics* indicate color photographs.

Acknowledgments

Recipes

Bruce Aidells
Francesca and Marchese Piero
  Antinori
John Ash
Mary Corpening Barber
Melanie Barnard
Nancy Verde Barr
Ed Behr
Anne Bianchi
Emily and Jon Biddle
Lena Cederham Birnbaum
Bistro Laurent, Paso Robles,
  California
Carole Bloom
Daniel Boulud
Deana and John Brainard
Georgeanne Brennan
Bill Brett
Giuliano Bugialli
Floyd Cardoz
Miriam Chandler
Bettina Ciacci
Lane Crowther
Lorenza de' Medici
Brooke Dojny
Emilio e Bona, Camaiore, Italy
Barbara Pool Fenzl
Charity Ferreira

Figs, Boston
Bobby Flay
Valeria Gambogi
Laura Gambrill
Rozanne Gold
Aviva Goldfarb
Darra Goldstein
Anne Graziano
Sophie Grigson
Ken Haedrich
Pam and Peck Hayne
Maida Heatter
Jennifer Hessler
Jack Fry's, Louisville, Kentucky
Cheryl Alters Jamison and
  Bill Jamison
Nancy Harmon Jenkins
Zov Karamardian
Jeanne Thiel Kelley
Kristine Kidd
Suzannah Knapp
La Bonne Étape,
  Château-Arnoux, France
Las Ventanas,
  Cabo San Lucas, Mexico
Michelle M. Littlefield
Larry Steven Londre
Susan Herrmann Loomis
Emily Luchetti
Lucia Luhan

Deborah Madison
The Mainstay Inn,
  Cape May, New Jersey
Michael McLaughlin
Selma Brown Morrow
Christine Piccin
Pizzeria Bianco, Phoenix
Stephan Pyles
Susan Quick
Steven Raichlen
Rick Rodgers
Betty Rosbottom
Cathy Sandrich
Chris Schlesinger
Cory Schreiber
Marie Simmons
Susan Fuller Slack
Sushi Roku, Los Angeles
Fabio Tani
Sarah Tenaglia
Beth and Tom Tiernan
Marcela Valladolid Rodriguez
Villa Mimosa, Bagnone, Italy
Bruce Weinstein
Jasper White
Sara Corpening Whiteford
Dede Wilson
Zuki Moon Noodles,
  Washington, D.C.
Randy Zweiban

Photography

Jack Andersen
E. J. Armstrong
Noel Barnhurst
David Bishop
Angie Norwood Browne
Daniel Clark
Wyatt Counts
Leo Gong
Charles Imstepf
Deborah Klesenski
Peter Langone
Michael La Riche
Brian Leatart
Jennifer Lévy
Carrie Lloyd
Gary Moss
Stephanie Rausser
Nancy Rosen
Jeff Sarpa
Rick Szczechowski
Mark Thomas